"A glorious and glossy, around-the-world look at the global sharing economy from the viewpoints of a diverse and inspiring group of young change-makers. Printed on sustainable paper, a percentage of each copy sold helps fund planting a tree and educating a slum girl in India. It educates, motivates and even agitates individuals and corporations into joining the sharing community in a beautiful way. Buy it. Read it. Love it. Share it. "

**DJ Paulette**

"If the vicious global pursuit of conspicuous consumption makes you despair, read Benita's book for some hope. "

**Mark Williams, actor**

"A marvellous and inspiring celebration of sharing across the world and across generations, written by one of the most knowledgeable and passionate authorities in the field. The stories gathered by the author are diverse, magical and heart-warming. "

**Patrick Andrews, social innovation lawyer**

**"** We have a saying in my house: 'Dream big and anything is possible'. The extraordinary people in this book aren't just dreaming but doing – against the odds to make their community and the world a better place. Illuminating, humbling and awe-inspiring. **"**

**Samantha Simmonds, TV news presenter and journalist**

**"** We all need inspiration and this book provides that much-needed shot in the arm to inspire and challenge. Buy it and share! **"**

**Lindsay Boswell, Chief Executive, FareShare**

**"** In a world filled with 'stuff' this inspirational book showcases how we can share knowledge, skills and resources for the benefit of all. **"**

**Oliver Heath, sustainable architectural and interior designer**

**"** Sharing is an essential part of social investment; this book helps us understand how. **"**

**Christine Gent, director of Fashion Revolution and People Tree, WFTO fair trade expert**

# Generation Share

First published in Great Britain in 2019 by

Policy Press
University of Bristol, 1-9 Old Park Hill, Bristol, BS2 8BB, UK
t: +44 (0)117 954 5940 | pp-info@bristol.ac.uk | www.policypress.co.uk

*North America office*:
Policy Press
c/o The University of Chicago Press, 1427 East 60th Street, Chicago,
IL 60637, USA
t: +1 773 702 7700 | f: +1 773-702-9756 | sales@press.uchicago.edu |
www.press.uchicago.edu

British Library Cataloguing in Publication Data
A catalogue record for this book is available from the British Library

Library of Congress Cataloging-in-Publication Data
A catalog record for this book has been requested

ISBN: 978-1-4473-5010-1 [PBK]
ISBN 978-1-4473-5038-5 [epdf]

Cover and text design by blu inc, Bristol
Printed and bound in Great Britain by Cambrian Printers, Aberystwyth
Policy Press uses environmentally responsible print partners

# Generation Share

The change-makers building the Sharing Economy

**BENITA MATOFSKA & SOPHIE SHEINWALD**

This book is dedicated to the brave Sharers everywhere who not only dare to dream of a better world, but who are boldly building it, overcoming great challenges in doing so. These tenacious, audacious change-makers demonstrate unequivocally the power of Sharing to transform our lives, our communities, our society, our economy and our planet. By reading this book, you are joining a global movement of people whose positivity and love for our planet, and all those who live in it, inspires hope for a brighter future.

**February 26th, 2017**

Dear Benita,

I hope my voice will reach you. My name is Aarti Naik, I'm a slum-based Young Girl Change-maker. I run Sakhi for Girls Education, a slum school for girls in Mumbai, India. We share knowledge and the chance of a positive future for girls. I would like to be part of your project because I am Generation Share. I strongly believe that because of you and your initiative, my slum-based girls' voices will reach globally!


I hope for the Best,

Aarti Naik

**"** *Generation Share* had just fully funded on Kickstarter and I was in a post-crowdfunding, exhausted state, when I received Aarti's message via LinkedIn. It made me stop and think. A girl, living in a slum, 5,000 miles away in Mumbai, had heard about the project and believed that by including her story in this book, it could make a difference. Perhaps the idea of showcasing positive stories of Sharing from around the world could achieve even more than I had hoped it would? **"**

**Benita Matofska**

My journey into the world of what has become known as the 'Sharing Economy' began during the turmoil of the 2008 financial crash. Like many, and at the expense of sounding like a complete cliché, I was reassessing my life. Following a 20-year successful career in television production, I wanted a change. The world that had once enthralled me now frustrated me. Fed up of predictable, reductive, formatted programmes that depicted an out of touch commissioner's bird's eye view of the world, I wanted to make a contribution, a real one. I took the leap and found myself a job in the charity sector, as the unlikely Head of Global Entrepreneurship for Enterprise UK, an organisation on a mission to inspire and equip young people, to have ideas and make them happen. My friends used to joke that my bombastic title sounded like I was 'Head of the World'.

It was thanks to my ridiculous job title that I was invited to be a 'counsellor' at the One Young World Congress in 2010. It was perhaps even more ridiculous that I ended up sharing a platform with Archbishop Desmond Tutu and Bob Geldof. Ridiculous maybe, but it was while standing on that platform, inspired by those around me who had made a significant contribution to end global poverty and apartheid, that I had my epiphany. Sharing. What the world needed to do was share. Following the One Young World Congress I couldn't sleep – for weeks. As the weeks turned into months, the word 'share' wouldn't leave me, so I quit my job and set off on my path of 'sharing'. Sharing what or how, I did not know, but I knew why and that was all that mattered. One morning, after a particularly restless night, I woke up and the first phrase that popped into my head was, 'what's wrong with the world is there's a shortage of sharing.' I went on to tell myself, 'we can fix that. If we find a way to unleash our unlimited power to share and collaborate, there's no end to what we can achieve.'

On 17 January 2011, I registered The People Who Share at Companies House, as a non-profit that helps people and organisations discover and participate in the Sharing Economy. The campaign to unleash our collective sharing potential was born.

Generation Share is the culmination of a decade long journey. A journey that has taken me around the world to meet some of the most inspiring people on the planet. A journey that has taught me, unequivocally, that the act of Sharing can, and is, changing our world. Three years ago, I decided that this journey had to be shared in the form of a book. In order to build a more caring, sharing society, we all deserve to know that this already exists. In cities, towns, villages, schools, communities, businesses, homes, streets, families, groups, individuals, hearts and minds; in every part of the world a Sharing Economy is growing. But unless you look for it, you may not see it. I wanted to make these human stories visible, to take people on a voyage of hope, to show, without doubt, the existence of Generation Share. Who better to join me on this journey than visual storyteller, photographer and dear friend Sophie Sheinwald? I knew that Sophie could capture the magic that these awe-inspiring Sharers are bringing to the world and transport them into your world so that they can show you the Sharing Economy is not a pipedream or a fantasy – it's a reality, and it's your reality too.

Aarti Naik's voice did reach me and, despite not having budgeted for a trip to India, in November 2017 Sophie and I travelled to Aarti's Sakhi school for slum-based girls in Mumbai. I hope that by sharing her incredible story and all the Generation Share stories, these voices of change will prove that not only is a society built around the sharing of human and physical resources possible, it's inevitable.

# CONTENTS

# OUR SPONSOR

**Angela Laws** is the 72-year-old social media and community manager at TrustedHousesitters, representing the heart and soul of this Sharing community. Angela has been with the company from the very beginning, combining her love for pet sitting with her full-time job. TrustedHousesitters is a membership-based house and pet sitting platform bringing together a worldwide community of home and pet owners and pet-loving sitters. Now in over 130 countries, TrustedHousesitters has helped make *Generation Share* possible by being our global sponsor.

" We're delighted to sponsor *Generation Share*, spreading the word that we are here to enable our community to share an exchange of value and trust.

Travelling owners share their homes and pets and, in doing so, pet lovers are able to travel more while pets stay happy at home. TrustedHousesitters is a unique platform, built on pure sharing. No money changes hands between members, it's a completely altruistic arrangement. That's the beauty of it. This is a community that builds friendships around the world, connecting like-minded animal lovers.

I started pet sitting as a way to heal after losing my beloved dog, Holly. My first sit was for a cocker spaniel, Charlie, who belonged to a young widow. She'd lost her husband to cancer and didn't want to put Charlie into kennels, so I looked after him while she went away on business. It was the most cathartic thing I had ever done. I wanted animals in my life, but I knew the time wasn't right for me to have another pet of my own. Sitting helped me find joy again.

Not long after, a young man called Andy Peck contacted me. He was starting TrustedHousesitters based on the idea that he would build a community of pet lovers that adored animals so much, they would care for them for free. Connecting with people just like me with a passion for animals, helping people and sharing trust – I had to be involved.

**TrustedHousesitters doesn't just help dog and cat owners, we help all creatures great and small. We share this planet with animals; we don't own it and we should look at them as beings to be kept safe, whether in the wild or at home. Animals impact our lives and are good for our health. Members of TrustedHousesitters tell us their lives have been turned around by the love of an animal.**

We can change both animal and human lives. For instance, sadly some families are separated – there are grandparents who would love to travel to see their grandchildren, but they also want to keep their pets happy at home. TrustedHousesitters enables them to do both.

Sharing through our community can change the way people think of others, too. For some, it's a leap of faith, but they soon realise this world is full of good people who want to connect and build trust. As one sitter said, 'they didn't just let us into their home, they also let us into their hearts and I will always remember the trust'.

Like so many members of our community I've been privileged to travel the world caring for pets, meeting wonderful people and creating lifelong friendships that would otherwise never have happened. "

## TrustedHousesitters™

trustedhousesitters.com

TRUSTEDHOUSESITTERS TEAM (L-R) (TOP) BALAZS HAJNAL (35), EILIDH HENDRY (27), FRANKIE KNIGHT (36), JIMMY TAYLOR (41), TIM RIJAVEC (32), WILL OGDEN (38), ANSSI JUNNOLA (30), PAUL MAISEY (40), ED LYON (31), ROB GREEN (37), CONOR ATKINSON (26), (MIDDLE) KAROLINA ANDRIJEVSKAYA (25), SOPHIE MAIN (25), INDIA COLES (24), LUKE PARKER (30), STEVE THOMSON (31), (BOTTOM) ELEANOR RUDGE (35), GEORGINA RICHARDSON (29), DUDLEY THE DOG, LISA LOGAN (44), LUCY BOTTING (27), ANGELA LAWS (72), BUSTER THE DOG, CHRIS GUY (28), NATHAN AYLWARD (24), ALEX CORNWELL (23), TASH RIJAVEE (34) AND QIROV THE DOG; ANGELA LAWS WITH BUSTER THE DOG.

> **"Our vision is that everybody who has pets or wants to spend time with them knows we are here so they can travel safely and affordably and enjoy life. We want to make this experience available for as many people and pets as possible, around the world."**

# WHAT IS THE SHARING ECONOMY?

**❝ Sharing means creating the conditions to understand others, it is not a one-way street, it isn't just giving something from my surplus to someone else, it's a relationship where somebody provides me with the opportunity to share with them. Sharing is a condition under which we can demonstrate a fundamental aspect of being human. You can discover what you have in common and where there are differences, through sharing, you can get to a point that you wouldn't without it. You cannot live without sharing. ❞**

**Alexandros Pagidas, sharer, philosopher, founder of Patreon**

*What does sharing mean to you?* When I interviewed Servane Mouazan, a social entrepreneur who helps women grow their social businesses, I asked her this question (as with every person interviewed for *this book*). She replied, 'Sharing is something bold, it's an engagement, it's a decision. There's nothing fluffy about sharing.' She's right, there isn't.

Of the 200 people interviewed for *Generation Share*, every single one had a different answer when asked that same question, confirming my view that the word 'sharing' means different things to different people; that in fact, there's a whole spectrum of Sharing. It is precisely that diversity that makes up what we call a 'Sharing Economy', a whole system based around the sharing of human and physical resources. *Generation Share* is a journey to meet the inspiring change-makers behind this phenomenon, but what exactly is the 'Sharing Economy'? What does it have to do with Sharing? And why has Sharing become *the* topic of our time?

There's nothing new about Sharing per se – it is as old as humanity itself. Hunter-gatherers were foraging and sharing food almost 2 million years ago in order to survive. These early human social networks (a precursor to the digital ones we have now) formed resilient economies based on cooperation and the most efficient use of available resources.[1] But the Sharing that was essential for our early evolution gave way to narcissism and eventually capitalism. By the end of the 20th century, competition and consumerism prevailed and the 'Happy Days'[2] of the 1950s, when sharing the proverbial sugar with a neighbour was commonplace, were over.

GROUP OF VOLUNTEERS WITH FOUNDER GIORGOS VALLIS AT
PALIOMYLOS ECO-COMMUNITY, EVIA, GREECE

The term 'Sharing Economy' emerged from the global crisis of 2008–09 and the need to do more with less. Its birth demonstrated that necessity is often the best mother of invention. Fuelled by technology that was able to match people who had spare or idle resources with those that wanted or needed them, the term became associated with new types of 'peer-to-peer' or person-to-person online marketplaces like Airbnb. In reality, the Sharing Economy is much more than a collection of new types of Silicon Valley backed ventures; it is wide-reaching and changing society as we know it. It is at once an economic system built around the sharing of human and physical resources and a mind-set. I define it simply:

## The Sharing Economy is a system to live by, where we care for people and planet and share available resources however we can.

Widely misunderstood, it's an umbrella term and includes different types of Sharing. Swap, borrow, exchange, collaborate, reuse, recycle, rent, vintage – all these terms refer to different types of Sharing. But how can renting someone's spare room be classified as 'Sharing'? If you are paying for something, where's the Sharing in that? Here's where it can get confusing. The 'Sharing' in a Sharing Economy doesn't necessarily mean it's free. Often, 'Sharing' refers to accessing a shared resource, such as when you pay to be a member of a car club. If we rent a shared item rather than buying it new and owning it outright, we are using fewer planetary resources, we have less of a negative impact as we only use what we need, we save money (access is cheaper than ownership) and we make social connections. If we buy vintage clothes, we are reusing a pre-existing resource – in both of these cases, we are 'sharing available resources', creating social impact, even though we are paying.

Money doesn't mean it's not a form of Sharing, though money does change things. How can it not? But that doesn't discount the Sharing and the positive impact that's created. So a Sharing Economy is known as a hybrid economy – sometimes you exchange money, sometimes you exchange something else. If you fix my laptop and I cook dinner for you, there's a value exchange, even if we're not paying with money as we know it. In this new economy, three types of value are recognised and counted – economic, social and environmental. All of this value exists in the world, often hidden; we don't usually account for it in any traditional sense. Yet we pay for it dearly. In the past three decades, in our haste to accumulate and own cars, electronics, clothes and white goods, we've consumed one-third of the planet's natural resources.[3] They're gone.

# So how does the Sharing Economy work and what's included?

The Sharing Economy is essentially made up of five parts:

## Categories
**what we share:** homes, goods, food, transport, skills, time, power, knowledge, responsibility.

## Subsets
**the broad spectrum of the Sharing Economy:** cooperatives, crowdsourcing, social enterprise, volunteering, fair trade, vintage.

## Mode
**how the Sharing happens in practice:** borrow, swap, exchange, rent, repair, recycle, collaborate, co-create, peer-to-peer.

## Characteristics & Values
**the qualities of the economy:** sustainable, transparent, inclusive, positive, circular, fair, compassionate.

## Impact
**why we share, the social impact created:** poverty reduction, social mobility, environmental protection, equality, community, wellbeing.

The Sharing Economy is essentially made up of five parts: verticals (what we share, which includes tangible resources such as food, and intangible resources such as knowledge); subsets – the divisions or parts that make up the spectrum of the Sharing Economy; mode (how the Sharing happens in practice); characteristics, and values and impact (why we share). By understanding what the Sharing Economy is we see that there's nothing fluffy about Sharing and its impact is significant. I'm passionate about Sharing because I'm certain it can change the world. I believe that what's wrong with the world is that there's a shortage of Sharing and we can fix that. For, although we live on a planet of finite resources, our potential to share is unlimited and if we can unleash our collective capacity to share, there is no end to what we can achieve.

40,000 people die each day because they don't have access to food, shelter or water.[4] The reality is we have enough food, shelter and water to feed, house and sustain all of them, *if* we can share our resources. And there's the rub. It's the Sharing that needs to happen and we are the ones that need to change. Sharing food, clothes and education means those 40,000 people who die each day wouldn't need to die. Yes, the magic of Sharing can transform our world and every single one of us has the power to make that change. The question is *how*?

So, *what is the Sharing Economy?* It's the system that makes the Sharing possible. It's *how* we will change the world.

But *Generation Share* isn't about the system, it's about the people who are creating the system and it's the people who share that have long been my interest. I wrote this book because I wanted to know *who* was behind the Sharing since this is a people's economy and it's the people (the Sharers) who are building it. Collectively, these are the human beings I call *Generation Share*. But who exactly are they? Are they young? Old? Rich? Poor? Women? Men? Non-binary? Disabled? Able bodied? Do they belong to or come from particular religions, ethnicities or cultures? Do they live in cities? Villages? Or on islands? Are they artists? Anarchists? Entrepreneurs? Or everyday folk just doing their best?

You only find things (or people) when you go looking for them. I went to look for *Generation Share,* for the brave, positive, change-makers. I wanted to document how these change-makers are saving and changing lives and evidence the power of Sharing to change the world. I intentionally sought out the positive stories, the stories of hope. Positivity is an important characteristic of the Sharing Economy because it provides a much-needed antidote to the disease of cynicism and negativity that is destroying our world. It's the language of this new economy. It offers people healing, hope and inspiration, much needed at a time when hate, totalitarianism and populism are winning votes. We have a global crisis of responsible leadership and to tackle our complex problems, we need solution-focused, socially conscious, but above all, positive leaders – change-makers. I believe, that by elevating the status of good, positivity and consciousness, we can begin to change our malfunctioning world.

GOLDEN HOUR AT PALIOMYLOS, EVIA, GREECE.

Perhaps positivity will lead us to a tipping point and these catalytic, small actions will create a 'butterfly effect'?[5] Seemingly, throughout history, small actions have instigated bigger change. So I decided to take a small action and go looking for Generation Share, because I believe in the power of positive stories and books to catalyse that bigger change. I invited a dear friend, visual storyteller and photographer Sophie Sheinwald, to join me so that we could discover the people behind the Sharing and, in turn, share the magic of our findings with you.

You could see this book as a series of eye-opening, individual human stories, brought to life through powerful imagery, each one told by the Sharer, in their own words. All are extracts from much longer interviews, recorded over the past three years in different parts of the world.[6] But their real impact is how, in combination, they tell the bigger story of the Sharing Economy. As Aristotle said, 'the whole is greater than the sum of its parts' or, in the words of Emilie Jacquetton, founder of health-sharing platform Ouiwin, "from the group of people that you never imagined knowing before comes the magic".

Each story is deliberately chosen because it contributes to that whole; you'll see by the colour it has been assigned that it represents one of the five features that make up the Sharing Economy. Some of Generation Share are founders, trailblazing social entrepreneurs who are educating slum kids or creating a food-sharing revolution to tackle food waste and poverty; some are micro-entrepreneurs or users of services that are change-makers themselves. For the Sharing Economy to function and thrive, you need both users and producers. Sharers trailblaze the use of the services, share the experiences, cause the ripples to occur. Others are included because they are intrapreneurs who chose jobs with large corporations, precisely so they can lead change from within. Then there are those selfless eco-community activists who, by leading sustainable lifestyles from the ground up, forge the way for others. These inspiring, positive, fearless, extraordinary, ordinary, creative, passionate, compassionate, ambitious, humble folk, en masse, make up the diversity, contradictions, beauty, potential and hope that really is the Sharing Economy.

Join us on a journey through this magical landscape. Your guides are the people who live, work and play in it. You will enter their worlds, their minds and their hearts; they will show you what Sharing means for them and perhaps in turn, you will be inspired and discover what it means for you.

Welcome to Generation Share.

OUISHAREFEST 2017, PANTIN, FRANCE.

# DOES AGE MATTER?

AV. RIBEIRA DAS NAUS, LISBON, PORTUGAL.

I n the beginning, the people creating the Sharing Economy and driving it (some quite literally) were millennials, most aged 25–34, middle class, educated, looking for experiences, adventure and a desire to belong. I called them 'Generation Share', a global peer group, connected via technology, united by sharing resources and driven by possibility.

**Research showed that of the world's 2.68 billion millennials, 73% saw the Sharing Economy as important to them,[7] preferring to access rather than own goods. With most Sharers having a degree or other qualifications and earning over \$100,000[8] a year, the Sharing Economy, it seemed, was a young thing, an educated thing and, most certainly, a middle-class thing.**

Fast forward to 2019 and 'Generation Share' has grown well beyond its early, hip, millennial adopters. Now over 28% of the global adult population are participating,[9] with 25% of Sharing Economy service providers being over 55.[10] Participation rates of over 55s on some sharing sites has grown over 375% in the past year[11] and adults aged 55–64 choosing renting, sharing and swapping over ownership has increased 80% in the past 12 years. Millennials may still form the largest group of Sharers, but the Sharing Economy has certainly spread outside of its earlier demographic leanings.

So is there a link between age and sharing? Does why, what and how we share vary as we age? When it comes to Sharing, does age matter?

# GENERATION Y (MILLENNIALS)

> ❝ Millennials think they can change the world, but they know they can't do this alone. They are connected from birth. They have the tools, mindset and passion to use technology for social good. ❞

**Inés Echevarria, crowdfunder, Barcelona**

They've been vilified and judged, they're the largest peer group in the US and India, and they've garnered more attention than any other generation. But go beyond the stereotypes and the tabloid headlines and you'll find that the global cohort first coined 'millennials' by William Strauss and Neil Howe,[12] (born between 1982 and 2004), brought us the 'Sharing Economy' in the first place. Millennials are natural born Sharers: they see that the road to consumption is paved with destruction; they recognise that the accumulation of stuff doesn't make us happier or healthier but brings heartache, for people and planet. They challenge the very ideas of ownership and utilisation. Why own a car when you only want a ride? Why stay in a hotel when you could live like a local? Why work solo when you could share a spare space? Access has fast become more of a status symbol than ownership, waste simply resource in the wrong place and the idea of paying for something you hardly use – downright foolish.

This generation not only recognises the importance of Sharing but sees anything else as pointless. They're smart, savvy and self-aware; 75% prefer to spend money on experiences rather than material possessions[13] and 30% have no interest in owning a car.[14] Their awareness extends well beyond themselves, often prioritising WE over ME, with nearly a third using Sharing Economy services and platforms for good causes.[15] And they're a trusting bunch, being three times more likely to have faith in each other than any other peer group.[16] Entrepreneurship is another millennial trait, with two-thirds choosing to freelance or work for themselves[17] and 70% saying sharing resources saves them time and money.[18] Millennials are the creators of the Sharing Economy and, of all age groups, the most excited by its potential.[19]

OUISHAREFEST 2017, PANTIN, FRANCE.

POONAM GAUTAM SHOWING HER SKILLS. (L TO R) DINESH CHANDER RATHOD, AJAY GURUNATH CHAVAN, OMKAR TALKAR, PRAKASH SAHANI, RAKESH SOMA RATHOD, AAMIR SHAIKH, SACHIN CHAVAN, RAJ KISHAN CHAVAN, VIJAY SHANTILAL CHAVAN, VIVEK RATHOD, SUJAL SINGHE, DEEPAK GUPTA, AMAN YADAV, ROHAN LOKHANDE, ASHOK RATHOD, SAGAR GOPAL RATHOD, OVAL GROUND, MUMBAI, INDIA.

# THE FOOTBALL SHARER

**Ashok Rathod is 29 years old and was born in one of Mumbai's biggest slums, Ambedkar Nagar. In 2006, he founded the *OSCAR Foundation* (Organisation for Social Change, Awareness and Responsibility), a social enterprise that provides after school programmes using football to attract, educate and empower underprivileged children. *OSCAR* has educated over 3,000 children.**

"Sharing means saving future generations; if we offer better education, children can grow up to be good human beings, making a positive contribution to the world.

When my best friend was 11, he dropped out of school to work. He spent his money on drinking, gambling and smoking. I was lucky, my father encouraged me to study. I saw two paths in life – to study and build a future, or drink, gamble and live in poverty. I knew I wanted to educate others that they had choices.

I learned football from the street, I learned teamwork and leadership. I realised I could address the issue of school dropouts. I saved up and bought a football for 400 rupees (£4). With one ball, I could help several children. At OSCAR, we give them an education in maths, English, IT and life skills. If they complete our classes, they can play football once a week and participate in competitions and camps. Our programme has 100% success rate. When I started, the school dropout rate was 55–60%, now it's 15–20%.

We are not asking them to change for us, we are asking them to change for themselves. If they don't want to, then OSCAR can't help them. One boy, Govind, dropped out of school at 11 because he wasn't getting enough food. He got a job in a restaurant where he could eat and get paid 600 rupees a month (£6). When he saw his friend playing football at OSCAR he wanted to play. I said, 'OK, but you have to go to school.' I enrolled him and now he is in Germany studying sports management at university."

" Football itself is sharing, because you can't play football alone – you need to pass the ball and share it. Through football, these children are getting an education, an opportunity to share their dreams, to have a future. I have a purpose in life, to share opportunities with young people so they can rise up from poverty. I don't focus on winning, I focus on win-win. Sometimes the kids say, 'oh no the match was a draw', 'penalty, penalty', and I say 'no penalty'. With no penalty, both teams win. In a win-win, everyone is happy. Sharing is win-win. "

ASHOK RATHOD WITH THE OSCAR FOUNDATION FOOTBALL TEAM, OVAL GROUND, MUMBAI.

# THE POETIC SHARER

" Many people in our generation are so caught up in being cool that they never open up. There's so much peer pressure, social pressure, success pressure that you end up being an embodiment of what pleases everyone else and lose yourself in being a façade for the public. The greatest gift that poetry gives us is we aren't the façade, we are able to share the truth that's behind it and young people want that sharing, we don't want a filter between us and others. Even in our darkest moments, we want someone to be around, to share our narrative. "

**LionHeart, poet and performer at Sofar Sounds**

LIONHEART (30) A POET FROM LONDON, PERFORMING AT SOFARSOUNDS, A SHARING PLATFORM THAT HOSTS GIGS IN UNDISCOVERED SPACES, FOLKLORE, HOXTON, LONDON.

LENA FASHION LIBRARY, AMSTERDAM, NETHERLANDS.

# THE FASHION SHARERS

**Juultje Dehing** is 28 years old and is part of the millennial team behind the *Lena Fashion Library* in Amsterdam, which attracts young women to borrow, rather than buy, clothes. She was born in the Netherlands.

**"** I'm passionate about making the right choices for the planet. When I was in school, we had to imagine future scenarios for the fashion industry. I read about the Sharing Economy and thought, 'Why isn't this happening in fashion?' It makes so much more sense. At Lena, we try to create a more sustainable way of consuming fashion to reach people who are not necessarily interested in sustainability by focusing on the fun part. You can experiment, you can wear everything once and not feel guilty, you just bring it back and switch it. You can come in daily and get a new outfit, or just use the library occasionally.

The collection we have is ours, like any library, and we give access to it. Sometimes people run into each other in the street and say 'Hey, you borrowed that from Lena, didn't you? I've worn that too.' That's the community benefit of a sharing system, because we all have access to this cool group of people that are members here.

The notion that consumption is based on ownership means that not only do you take from the environment, but also your closet space and your house gets full of stuff you don't wear or use, because we are programmed to want new things. But if we get rid of ownership, and you just pay for what you use, then it releases you of clutter and lowers the planetary impact. There's still a need for some ownership, so you have a good collection of clothes that you invest in, things that you will wear for a long time. So if you want something new, or you want to try a different style, you can come here and do that. This is the playful way of consuming fashion.

Sharing is selflessness. Just because I want to look good and express my individuality in my clothing doesn't mean I have to own it. It's more freeing, I don't need to grab something, take it, and own it, so no one else can. I can share it instead. **"**

> **"** We are used to renting books, but the idea that we can borrow clothes is something new. I love the idea that you can share your personal style too – that's exciting. **"**
>
> **Jule Jung, member of the Lena Fashion Library**

JULE JUNG (34) FROM KOREA, BORROWING CLOTHES, LENA FASHION LIBRARY, AMSTERDAM, NETHERLANDS.

# THE SKILLS SHARER

❝ When you share skills, what you receive in return does not necessarily have to come from the same person that you shared with. There's a 'butterfly effect' and once you share skills, you are part of a universal, never-ending circle of sharing. Some call it karma. ❞

**Maria Inês Nunes, skills sharer, Portugal**

MARIA INÊS NUNES (20), SKILLS SHARER, LER DEVAGAR BOOK HUB, LX FACTORY LISBON.

# THE SOCIAL SHARER

❝The Social Bar builds relationships and community. People were working in silos, we wanted to create a place where they could come and break the norms. Whatever age you are, you understand that the social mask we've all been wearing has to be removed. Maybe it's easier for young people to share because our lives are more fluid and we aren't set in our ways yet.❞

**Maeva Turdo, creator, Social Bar**

MAEVA TURDO (32), CREATOR OF THE SOCIAL BAR IN GARE DE LYON, PARIS, THAT USES A CHALLENGE BOX TO FACILITATE MEANINGFUL CONNECTIONS BETWEEN PEOPLE.

LES DEFIS
DU SOCIAL BAR

APOSTOLOS SIANOS AT FREE AND REAL, EVIA, GREECE.

# THE FREEDOM SHARERS

**Apostolos Sianos** is 37 years old and established *Free and Real*, a sustainable eco-community on the island of Evia in Greece. The community offers an alternative lifestyle and is attracting millennials from different parts of the globe.

" Free and Real is an acronym. It stands for Freedom of Resources for Everyone, Everywhere, Respect, Equality, Awareness and Learning. The ultimate goal is a resource-based economy for the entire human race. In the past six and a half years, more than 20,000 people have come here from all over the world to live differently.

I never really liked what I saw growing up. I figured out that endless consumption and growth does not make sense. I was working as a designer, earning a good salary, but I did not have a life. I was constantly working and on call. So I quit my job and left my house in Athens. A group of us created Free and Real. Here, we are focused on sharing.

Our motto is 'sharing is everything'. We are a bubble inside the capitalist system, but this project gives young Greeks an opportunity to escape the black hole of Athens and offer an alternative.

For me, sharing is the next evolution of our economy. Growing up, I used to watch *Star Trek*, which is basically a society that has abandoned a monetary system, where everyone works for the improvement of humankind. Even though it is a fantasy, I have seen these principles work here. I prefer to live in a place where everyone does what they do because they like to do it. Together, you can help expand human knowledge and civilisation. "

FREE AND REAL: MARIA, CROC PLANTER, SIGN OF VALUES, EVIA, GREECE.

**F**reedom of
**R**esources for
**E**veryone,
**E**verywhere
**&**
**R**espect,
**E**quality,
**A**wareness and
**L**earning

Maria **(20)** cooks for the community at Free and Real in Evia, Greece.

❝ When I was 16 years old, I realised that community and traditions meant everything to me. I wasn't comfortable with life, I couldn't be who I wanted. I was searching for a different way of life, to find a place that would match my beliefs. Eventually, I found Free and Real. Here, I don't have to explain myself or say what my beliefs are, because everyone shares the same values. It feels like home and it's what I want to do for the rest of my life. ❞

# CO-LIVING

66 More than 500 people live here; the youngest is 18, the oldest is 66. You get to experience people in different ways, not just in the workplace but where they feel at home. We take it in turns to cook, we're all different nationalities. I'm Nigerian, there's Ayub who is Moroccan and Nick's from Manchester. Nick and I host a regular party here and we encourage everyone to get involved, it's a way of getting people together from different walks of life. You realise that we may have different backgrounds, but we are all human. People would be a lot more tolerant if co-living was more widespread in the world. 99

**Francis Okolie, member of The Collective**

WORK, REST AND PLAY: (MAIN IMAGE) FRANCIS OKOLIE (27) AT THE BAR; (TOP RIGHT) EXTERIOR, (BOTTOM RIGHT) CO-WORKING SPACE AND LOBBY, THE COLLECTIVE, THE LARGEST CO-LIVING AND WORKING SPACE IN LONDON, UK.

# GENERATION X

Misunderstood, misquoted, misattributed, even the true origins[20] of the moniker 'Generation X' have been misrepresented. First used by Robert Capa in 1953 for a post-war, coming of age photo essay, later adopted by Brit punk artist Billy Idol for his 1976 band, the term eventually made its way into the mainstream when Douglas Coupland popularised it in his 1991 book *Generation X: Tales for an Accelerated Culture*. But despite being labelled 'slackers', defined by divorce and given latchkey kid status, the cohort born between 1965 and 1984 are much more than lazy rebels – particularly when it comes to Sharing.

Having witnessed key world events, Generation X's personal and political experiences have enabled them to lead the biggest societal shifts of the last four decades. From tech, to innovation and pop culture itself, this is the generation that brought us the internet. Gen X's socially progressive mores, along with their punk, DIY culture, laid the foundations for today's Maker Movement and kick-started current political activism as we know it.

Their 'work hard, play hard' mentality reveals an entrepreneurial spirit that is at the heart of the Sharing Economy. More than half of start-up founders are Gen-Xers, with this peer group more likely than any other to start a business.[21] They consider themselves entrepreneurs,[22] and make up 38% of the micro-entrepreneurial providers that fuel the Sharing Economy.[23] If you combine this with resourcefulness, independence and self-sufficiency, it's not surprising that their attitude to work has spawned the sub-set of the Sharing Economy known as the 'gig economy'. 21% view workplace flexibility as top priority and are likely to walk away from their current job if this is unavailable.[24]

Gen-Xers are the first group of peers to become high-tech parents and the last to have a low-tech childhood. They represent the shift from a manufacturing to a service economy. Having proven their ability to care for parents and children simultaneously, this 'sandwich generation'[25] has journeyed far from its Breakfast Club slacker origins.[26] Their rejection of social norms and authority, and their questioning of consumer capitalist society, has given them the skills to build a new, fairer, smarter economy based around the creation of economic, social and environmental value, putting people and planet at its heart.

**To understand this generation is to understand the Sharing Economy. The millennial love child could not have created it without the life lessons of their Gen X parents. Yes, millennials may have conceived the Sharing Economy, but Generation X will sustain it.**

SHARING A MOMENT: RIO MARAVILHA, LX FACTORY, LISBON, PORTUGAL.

# THE CARING SHARERS

**Coen van de Steeg** is **46** years old and was born in the Netherlands. He is the founder of *WeHelpen*, a Sharing platform connecting those who need help with those who offer it.

**Astrid Farhuten** is **50** years old and was struggling to cope with the special needs of her child and her elderly mother, Sjaan van Coolwÿk, so she turned to *WeHelpen*.

**Sjaan van Coolwÿk** (known as Mrs Kok) is **84** years old, she now receives the practical help and support she needs.

**Tineke Mueler** is **48** years old and, as a *WeHelpen* volunteer, visits Mrs Kok regularly.

"**Coen:** I was a director in digital technology, then I was hit by a car and woke up in intensive care with a brain injury. My wife became a carer overnight. After three years she collapsed. I thought, 'What do I need to do to change the situation I am in now?' The doctor told me that taking hikes would be good for my brain injury. I thought, 'If I'm going to be outside, I could walk someone's dog who has a broken hip, but how do I find them?' I dreamed up an app where I could offer and receive help. Our social capital is hidden, because people, especially young people, don't see themselves as traditional volunteers, but they are open to doing something, in a new way. We have to make social capital visible. Everyone has value and can contribute to society, we all need help someday, either for ourselves or for someone else. That's when WeHelpen was born.

**Astrid:** I wanted my mother to have more support, so she could really enjoy life. I now have a care schedule for her by using WeHelpen. It's a big relief and I have time to rest. On Thursdays, Tineke is always here, so I know that my mother will eat and be looked after. I don't only depend on institutions. Previously, my mother had accidents, but now there's a safety net. It goes two ways, I can talk to Tineke about my mother's health, she understands what's happening. My mother talks about Tineke all the time and thinks of her as another daughter – her favourite daughter now!!!

" We hope that this movement (we see WeHelpen as a movement) leads to social consciousness that helping each other becomes a natural thing to do. Currently, people don't want to share their vulnerability, it's harder to say you need something, it's easier to say 'I can share something', it makes you more in control. You are more equal to others if you can say 'I have something to offer'. If you don't it's hard to have confidence. Sharing is about self-confidence. "

**Coen van de Steeg, founder, WeHelpen**

COEN VAN DE STEEG AT DE
STOOTERSPLAS LAKE, WHERE HE WAS
INSPIRED TO CREATE WEHELPEN,
NETHERLANDS.

**Tineke:** My own mother was living alone; as I don't live nearby, I wanted to find someone local who could visit her. Then I thought, maybe there is someone who lives near me who is also alone and who needs help. So I looked online and discovered WeHelpen – that's how I met Mrs Kok.

**Mrs Kok:** Tineke is more like part of the family. There's a great connection between the two of us, she makes me feel comfortable and safe.

**Tineke:** Mrs Kok always asks me about my mother and that makes me feel good because she's also interested in me. I have the time, because I'm not working that often, my children are growing up and they don't need me as much. To care for someone else makes me feel wanted.

**Mrs Kok:** When you share, age doesn't matter, sometimes I feel like I'm 18! Sharing is about how you interact. I want to participate in life, to dance, sing, to make a contribution! It's important that you can share good times with others, it's the essence of life.

**Mrs Kok:** Before Tineke started coming to visit me, I had an accident, I fell and was laying on the ground screaming for 5 hours. Now I have help in my life, so the impact of sharing is life-changing. I have more confidence, I feel safe, valued and I can continue living here.

**Astrid:** This is so important for the whole system. The costs of healthcare are very high, so when people can stay longer in their own homes, instead of bringing them to a home for the elderly, they can be in their own environment, where the help comes to them, they can have a better quality of life, and it's less costly.

**Coen:** We want to empower everyone, young and old, to think about what they can share, what they can give back to society. We live in a society with an ageing population and thanks to innovation and technology, we can live longer. As we grow older, we still have value, we just need to make that visible and possible for people to use and know that value.

Older people are raised with the mindset that you keep the dirty laundry inside, that you don't need any help; younger people know this isn't the case, there's a very promising generation yet to come. 〞

MUTUAL ADORATION: (L TO R) TINEKE MUELER, SJAAN VAN COOLWŸK AND ASTRID FARHUTEN, AT SJAAN'S HOME IN OOSTZAAN, NETHERLANDS.

# THE RECYCLER

**❝** Sharing is about discovering the abundance within and around oneself. In my everyday life, I access what I need and give away what I don't, through a human network of neighbours, friends and family across generations. The Sharing Economy enables me to connect with available resources. I recently moved and had to rebuild an apartment. I wanted to reuse existing materials, to reduce the use of natural resources and money. By relying on my network, I received so many personalised items, all with their own story. It turned into a collaborative project! My 80-year-old neighbour, who has 50 years of experience in art exhibitions, gave me a chair and advised me on decor. **❞**

**Candida Rato, eco-consultant and Sharing Economy promoter, Portugal**

CANIDA RATO (37), AN ECO-CONSULTANT AND PROMOTER OF THE SHARING ECONOMY AT HER HOME IN LISBON, PORTUGAL.

# THE SHAREPRENEUR

**Saasha Celestial-One** is the 41-year-old American co-founder of *Olio*, a food-sharing app that connects neighbours with each other and with local businesses so that no good food goes to waste. Through *Olio*, Saasha is starting what she calls, a 'food sharing revolution'.

" My parents were big hippies, baby boomers. I grew up poor and spent my childhood following my mum around collecting things that could be salvaged, repurposed and sold. The idea of giving things a second chance is in my DNA. I was not going to spend my adult life without security, so I set up a bullet-proof CV by working at a lot of global corporate firms, but when I was on maternity leave, I knew I couldn't leave my kid and do work that was not meaningful.

I teamed up with Tessa, the daughter of dairy farmers from Yorkshire who grew up learning how much hard work goes into preparing our food. When I found out how much food goes to waste, I was horrified. It seemed a massive inefficiency that could be tackled through technology. Food waste is the third largest contributor to climate change and one of the most pressing problems affecting mankind. So we founded Olio, a sharing platform for food. 'Olio' is a synonym for 'hodgepodge', a mixture of things.

Olio is having a massive social impact; we have 1,000,000 users globally who have collectively shared almost half a million portions of food and over 16,000 volunteers. We know that of the people that request food, 40% are households living below the poverty line and we get emails telling us that they would not have had a meal if it weren't for Olio. 8.2 million people are food insecure, these are the people who are benefitting from Olio, the hidden hungry.

Our big vision is to connect everyone, so that we are all well fed. If we could displace 5–10% of new purchases at supermarkets, the downstream impact would be phenomenal for the environment. The big vision is to build an established secondary market for food. Currently, our consumption takes place in the primary market, in supermarkets. If there is a viable secondary market that eliminates food waste and starts to displace the purchasing of food from the primary market then the demand for food shrinks, less goes to landfill, and it frees up a lot of resources that go into making the food.

**25% of the world's water supply is used for food that is never eaten. If we free these resources to do something productive for humanity, we could end world hunger. "**

---

SAASHA CELESTIAL-ONE RECEIVING SURPLUS FOOD, NORTH LONDON, UK.

# THE DIGITAL NOMAD

**Deborah Simmons** is 41 years old and from London. She is participating in *Remote Year*, a Sharing initiative which brings communities of professionals, entrepreneurs and freelancers from around the world to spend a year together, as part of a shared living, working, travelling community.

" I was feeling discontented with my life, I wanted to travel, but after four years building up my business, it felt irresponsible to just up sticks and desert my clients. Then I discovered 'Remote Year' where you travel for a year with a community, living in a different place each month. Everybody has their own work, you share accommodation, workspace and have the opportunity to have a positive social impact in each place. So... I became a digital nomad; travelling and working alongside a sharing community where a laptop, phone and decent Wi-Fi are really all you need to sustain the lifestyle. There are 58 in our community and we have an amazing pool of combined resources: software developers, lawyers, graphic designers, writers... I am a strategic consumer insight consultant.

We all stayed in the same accommodation last month, and we had one broom between 58 of us, so we had to dedicate an online channel to share the broom!! We are each other's family when we are here. You share your space, your experiences... you make dinner for each other. We have tiny fridges here and food is expensive; if I buy a whole carton of milk I know I won't use it so I'll share it with a friend to avoid waste.

I'm aware it's a bit of a bubble, but in my bubble it's amazing to be with a community of people who are motivated and excited about life. And every month we organise a social impact project so that we can leave a positive imprint wherever we go. In Belgrade we met two women running a charity to support the homeless. They had a website but no 'donate' button so they couldn't accept donations online. We fixed that. Tomorrow we are installing a water tank for a local community.

Remote Year shows that there's another way. You don't have to work for 50 years to then be able to enjoy life – you never know how things are going to turn out. This journey gives you the most amazing shared experiences and enables you to be part of a global sharing community. I'm still trying to figure out the right term for it... people ask, 'What are you doing? Are you working? Travelling? Living? What are you doing?' We're sharing! "

DEBORAH SIMMONS CO-WORKING, PÚBLICO, MEXICO CITY, MEXICO.

# FAMILIES, KIDS AND GENERATION Z

As the world changes, families change; the mythical nuclear household fashioned in the 1950s remains only in obsolete ads. It has given way to the blended, diverse, 21st century modern family that would make Jay Pritchett proud.[27] With extended adolescence, the ages for marriage and childbirth on the increase and 'relay' or 'tag-team' parenting, families are now multifarious juggling collectives, where individual needs are catered for and nothing is cookie-cutter.

With these seismic familial shifts, comes the challenge of the breakdown of traditional family roles. In India, Procter & Gamble caused a stir with their #Sharetheload Ariel detergent campaign, depicting a father apologising to his daughter for being a poor role model by not sharing the housework. But while the structure of the family and the world around it may have changed, what it means to be a family hasn't.

Resource scarcity, the need to do more with less and a return to community values make the Sharing Economy an attractive proposition for families. It's out with the new and in with the old, as eco-friendly kids' clothing, reusable diapers, vintage fashion and sustainable fabrics are having a resurgence.

These new kids on the block are known as 'Generation Z', and they were literally born to share. Whereas their parents choose access over ownership and millennials choose experiences over ownership, Generation Z juggle multiple experiences often simultaneously. They joined the planet between 1996 and 2019 and are expected to reach 2.56 billion (or 33% of the population) globally by 2020.[28] This post-millennial, digital native cohort has no knowledge of a world without Wi-Fi, smart phones or YouTube. They multi-task across five screens a day[29] and are so screen-addicted that 40% say working Wi-Fi is more important than a working toilet.[30] Theirs is a world of incessant updates and, despite their much chided attention span of eight seconds (goldfish have the accolade of nine), this means they're able to process information faster than any other generation, emulating the very machines they spend six hours a day on.[31]

With exposure to endless information and choices, they have high standards and won't settle for 'good enough', making Gen Z a demanding lot. It is this persistence, combined with a drive to change the world, plus the knowledge and entrepreneurial know-how, that makes Gen Z the Sharing Economy's best asset. Determined to contribute,[32] 76% are concerned about our human impact on the planet[33] and 26% share their time by volunteering.[34] Some are carers, raised in households with grandparents, giving them respect for the elderly. Most see themselves as global citizens, concerned about children dying of preventable diseases and world hunger. The most open-minded bunch to date, they live multiculturalism and diversity, have one or more friends from a different race and sexual orientation.[35] What's more, older Gen Z-ers are taking these values into the workplace with many asserting that company diversity affects their choice of gig.[36]

This is a generation of social entrepreneurs (one of the most popular career choices), collaborative team players, who like to share knowledge[37] and believe that brands and businesses can change the world. 92% say a company's social impact would affect their decision to work there, 61% consider getting new experiences more important than climbing the corporate ladder, and 70% would rather share information with their pet than their boss.[38]

Technology has forever changed not only how families communicate, but how they live, work and play. In this 24/7, on-demand, screen-obsessed era, we are exposed to more information in one day than our predecessors experienced in a lifetime. For Gen Z, the Sharing Economy is *the* economy – as much a part of them, as they are of it and so innate they may not realise it. And ... it is they who will take it mainstream.

ITS HIN (4), AT HOME PLAYING WITH RESHOPPER TOYS, AMSTERDAM, NETHERLANDS.

# THE MUMPRENEUR

**"** There are a lot of inspiring, creative and entrepreneurial women who've found a way to juggle both being a mum and having a career. Being a mumpreneur gives you license to say this is who I am, this is what I'm doing, you are a mum, but as a mumpreneur, you share yourself. You have to take a lot of risks, be courageous and caring because you have to put the needs of that little person ahead of yourself. That marries with the Sharing Economy, because you are putting yourself and others at the forefront. **"**

**Jane Robbie, mumpreneur**

JANE ROBBIE (47) WITH 10-YEAR-OLD SON KYE AT JANE'S PLACE, A SHARED COMMUNITY SPACE IN HER HOME, HOVE, SUSSEX.

(L TO R) LIVIA (11) AND JASMINE VAN RYSEWYK (9), SAMANTHA VAN DEN BOS (31), EVA (7) AND ROEL VAN RYSEWYK (44), IN THEIR AMSTERDAM HOME.

# THE SHARING FAMILY

❝ This whole concept of the nuclear family is flawed. Actually, family is also your friends, neighbours and other people, it's a network. It takes a village to raise kids. One of the first things Samantha told me when we met was 'Roel, we will not go nuclear!' I understood what she meant! Sharing is what families do, sharing space, sharing blood, sharing friendship, sharing love, sharing food and sharing the washing up – that's family! ❞

**Roel van Rysewyk, who along with his family live their lives through the Sharing Economy**

# THE KIDS WHO SHARE

❝One time, I found a really cool skipping rope. I was super happy because I didn't have one, so I could practice my skipping. Recently, I had a competition and thanks to the 'share house', I became really good at it. I skipped 130 times and got a certificate!❞

**Nanou van Sprang**

❝I also really like the fact that by sharing things, we help the environment. It makes me happy that I can put things there that I don't need and make somebody else happy.❞

**Roelie van Sprang, who with her sister Nanou set up the Share House outside their home in Amsterdam**

ROELIE (10) AND NANOU VAN SPRANG (7) AT THE 'SHARE HOUSE' OUTSIDE THEIR AMSTERDAM APARTMENT.

# THE TOY SHARER

**"** By sharing and using toys for longer, it saves in multiple ways. It saves you money, energy and also helps the environment. Most people don't realise that manufacturing new clothes and toys needs energy and water, so if you throw them away, all those resources are wasted. Sharing kids' stuff is especially important, because it's a lot of plastic and if you just throw it away, it goes to landfill. My kids get to know what sharing their stuff really means. I hope for future generations it becomes normal to share toys rather than buy them new. **"**

**Ellemieke Hin, user of Reshopper**

ELLEMIEKE HIN (39) WITH HER SON ITS (4), AN ACTIVE USER ON TOY-SHARING PLATFORM, RESHOPPER, AT HOME IN AMSTERDAM.

# THE HOUSE SWAPPERS

" House swapping makes travelling much easier, because we're staying in other people's homes where they have lots of toys, which are more valuable to the children than room service! Swapping homes is like sharing our lives. You see how a family lives; it's swapping almost everything. I'm letting someone sleep in my bed, use my bathroom. I never thought I'd do this, but we have discovered a whole new world and get to travel an extra time each year because it's cheaper. "

**Sergi Martin, regular house swapper with Knok platform**

REGULAR HOUSE SWAPPERS WITH SHARING PLATFORM KNOK, (L TO R) ROC (5), BRUNA (3), DOLO GUITART (36) AND SERGI MARTIN (46) AT THEIR HOME, BARCELONA, SPAIN.

# THE MILK SHARERS

**Dr Natalie Shenker** is 39 years old and with co-founder Gillian Weaver established *Hearts Milk Bank*, the first human breast milk bank in the UK.

**Jessie Hollet** is 31 years old and from the UK; she has two children – 8-month-old baby Austin and 3-year-old Isaac – and shares her breast milk.

**Silke Durm** is 42 years old and from Germany; she volunteers at the milk bank. She believes her son Felix owes his life to the sharing of breast milk.

**"Dr Natalie Shenker:** I realised that there was an acute problem with milk banking of hospitals having access to a supply of donor milk, even though there were hundreds of women who wanted to donate their milk. Over the last 18 months, I've established the first human milk bank in the UK and we aim to be not only a clinical provider, but also a place of research so we can carry out breast cancer research and examine different ways donor milk can be used with premature babies. We operate like the blood transfusion service. Milk is donated to us, we screen the donors for infectious diseases or any lifestyle issues that might compromise the milk going to vulnerable or sick babies. We operate according to nationally agreed guidelines to make sure that safety is fundamental to everything we do and then we process milk and provide it to hospitals and neonatal units.

**Jesse**: If I can take pressure off just one mum who has a premature baby to make that experience as best and easy as it can be, then why wouldn't I? I've got all this extra milk. My toddler who is three, likes to help me, so he gets the bottles out of the cupboard and he'll say, 'Mummy's sharing milk out of her boobies for the poorly babies'. I love that my three-year-old knows that I'm sharing and that encourages him to share. My kids think sharing is just what people do, it's as natural as saying 'please' and 'thank you'. It's easy to say that's mine or I want all of this, but it takes a bigger person to say, I'm enjoying this, maybe somebody can share this with me? If I can instil that in both my boys now, then hopefully they'll take this into their life.

EVERY DROP COUNTS: DR NATALIE SHENKER AT HEARTS MILK BANK.

**Silke:** Sharing has changed my life dramatically because sharing milk saved my son Felix's life. He was born premature at 28 weeks, he was very little and could not be breast fed by me as my own milk didn't come in straight away. We were lucky that we happened to be in a hospital where they offered donor milk, which meant that my son who was at risk of getting infections because his own immune system wasn't developed yet, could have the chance of receiving the next best thing to my own milk.

**Jesse:** It's so easy to share milk – it's probably easier than giving blood and people do that ten-fold. It takes me 5 minutes to make one bottle and I share 15 bottles a month. My monthly bottles could feed a poorly baby for over two weeks – it blows my mind a little bit. Sharing my milk makes me feel proud as a mum, it makes me feel proud as a human that there is such a lot of negativity in the world at the moment and if everyone could just do one thing, even if this is just my one thing that I do, I could look back and know that I definitely helped somewhere. Every time I look at Austin and look back on my breast feeding experience, I'll remember this amazing bonding experience and now, I've got this to add to that. I can think 'wow, not only did I feed him, but I fed at least one other baby'.

**❝ You have to imagine you are in an ICU unit, your child is in an incubator, there are tubes and cables everywhere and he can't even breathe by himself. Knowing that my baby still could be fed by donor milk was the moment I thought I'm so thankful that somebody took the time to share their milk, it came through a chain of people who were willing to share. We need to get back to that and not be so engrossed in our own lives. All women who are able to share their milk are heroes to me. ❞**

**Silke Durm, volunteer, Hearts Milk Bank**

**Natalie:** The whole of society could benefit from milk banks scaling if human milk was used exclusively across the NHS and neo natal care units. A report showed this could save about £47 million in care costs every year and £130 million in productivity loses. Families fall apart when babies are in intensive care; the divorce rate is phenomenal – it's recorded at over 50% for any baby that's in hospital for any length of time due to the stress that families go through. If we can offset that by however much, then it's worth it. "

L TO R: VOLUNTEER SILKE DURM; DONOR JESSIE HOLLET WITH BABY AUSTIN; BABY AUSTIN; VOLUNTEER MILK COURIER DAVID WILSON, WELWYN, UK.

# SHARING IT ALL

**Gina Farish** was born in the USA and is 42 years old. She's the Founder of *Sharemrkt*, an online network marketplace that seeks to bring the Sharing Economy together in one place.

" My husband, King, and I are always moving and wanting to see new places, experience new things. We live very light which gives us flexibility to travel or move without being inhibited by material things. When our son Whalen was born, we just continued that. As a family, engaging in the Sharing Economy has enabled us to live life how we want to live it.

Sharemrkt is a network-based platform that is more cooperative in nature, where you can find all of the sharing service providers in one place. I realised that there were thousands of them, yet you couldn't find them because they were fragmented and separate. I spotted a start-up need. I saw that via technology, there was an incredible opportunity for people to live where they want, do what they love and make a living out of it.

We want to raise Whalen with a true sense of gratitude. Living in a first-world country, things are very easy. It's sometimes difficult to teach and embed those core values of being grateful. Having a personal exchange when he is giving his toys and sharing with someone else and going out and picking his other things, he knows it came from someone else and it starts to change your mindset. So it's, 'OK, I finished this book, who would like this book?' That is one of the reasons why I am grateful to the Sharing Economy.

Different generations are more familiar with different forms of exchange, but sharing is across every age. It really comes back to openness. There's no age differentiation on who can engage or who should be engaged. You are never too old or young to share. "

GINA FARISH WITH SON WHALEN, GRÀCIA, BARCELONA, SPAIN.

**"** My dream is that you can do everything you would normally do through the Sharing Economy and you don't know that you are doing it through the Sharing Economy because it's just your life and it is easy. You can borrow a car or a home, or find a job, make a meal, connect with a community. All of these exchanges are very personal because you are connected with tools where you are really trusting someone or someone is really trusting you, and to me, it is like trusting the world. That's what I want to achieve through Sharemrkt. **"**

YOUTH MATTERS: PREQUEL CAMPAIGNERS, BRIGHTON YOUTH CENTRE (BYC), (L TO R) TILLY WILSON, BETTE DAVIS AND MONTY ANDERSON.

# GENERATION Z

Monty Anderson (16), Tilly Wilson (17) and Bette Davis (17) are from Brighton in the UK and belong to *Prequel*, a campaigning group that takes on issues relevant to young people. They often spend time at Brighton Youth Centre (BYC). Mike Roe (54) is the Director of BYC.

" **Monty:** One of my favourite things to share is communal spaces. I spend a lot of time in the youth centre and no one really owns it. It is kind of trash but we all want to live here. We take collective responsibility. It is in a sort of perfect state.

**Bette:** We like the fact that there's pizza on the walls and each one of them is a shared memory that we cherish.

**Monty:** Prequel was set up as a youth-led, horizontally-oriented, direct-action organisation.

**Bette:** It turned into a way for young people to have a voice. Whenever we have meetings, we decide who will chair that meeting. No one is more important than anyone else.

**Monty:** We share the burden of activism, the direct action. Political parties revolve so much around one single person yet humans are really flawed. When you have collective groups that have collective views, rather than the views of an individual, you can get better results, because you are not relying on one single person's morality, you are relying on a group.

**Bette:** I think everyone should share public spaces. There was the Public Space Protection Order (PSPO) which would fine homeless people for sleeping in public spaces. Prequel realised that was not a good thing and that we should share the space that people live in.

**Monty:** I think it is not permanent to own land. I could own this house for a bit and after I die someone else has to come and live here. It's not like I own a car but, if I did, I'd own a car for a few hours for a trip to London.

**Bette:** People feel like they own things once they have bought them with money. So, I own these shoes because I went out and paid for them, but I would not say that someone owns the park. No one owns the sea.

SOCIAL SPACE, BYC, BRIGHTON, UK.

**Monty:** Personally, I don't aspire to own, as long as I have some place to live and I am happy. I don't need a load of things to fulfil that.

**Mike:** I like to own guitars and share them. I am happy to share cars but I covet my motorbike as an object. But, who owns the Youth Club? It's not because you pay for it, but because you belong to it and it belongs to you, I am fascinated by it.

**Monty:** What is it that makes people share? Is it as kids, you are forced to share and once they become adults they say, 'I have shared my entire life, now I want to own things.' Maybe, that is why we aspire to own clothes and other things? Maybe as children we were forced to share it all. Social media ruins the natural part of sharing. In real life, you have to live with yourself. It is nice to know that everyone is distinct but on social media, people make any sort of life they want. If you look at my profile, you would get a very polished view of me, with the abrasive part removed. The most interesting and best parts are those that are raw, natural and authentic. I love Snapchat because it is so much more human, more fleeting. One of the things about social media is that things remain there. What I like about verbal talking is that it is fleeting and it cannot be used against me in the same way.

**Bette:** Why would you want to share the grimy part of yourselves to literally hundreds and thousands of people? It is like memories. You do not want to remember the really bad memories. So, you only document the good stuff because that is what you want to remember.

**Monty:** I hope that sharing will entirely reshape society and we will no longer rely on this model of being rented by someone to work, in order to rent land and then live. I wonder if we could just cooperatively share labour. It would be the sort of end of the capitalist cycle and it would be sustainable. The economy I'd like to see is no economy. In some areas, we have complete abundance but it is artificially kept scarce. I wonder if we could almost get rid of economies entirely. We have so much food and so much technology, we're on the brink of automating production. We do not need an economy at all.

**Bette:** I feel the question of what type of economy I would like to see is too big a question for one person to answer in an art room. I don't know. A nice one where people are treated equally, where people can get on?

**Monty:** I hope that there could be large-scale societal change in my lifetime. So I am not thinking so much about climbing up in my career ladder, rather, will others be able to start and reshape societies for everyone? 🎙️

YOUTH STRIKE 4 CLIMATE, BRIGHTON, FEB 15TH 2019; SKATE PARK; SOCIAL SPACE, BYC, BRIGHTON, UK.

# GENERATION BOOMER

When, nine months after the end of the Second World War, 'the cry of the baby was heard across the land',[39] baby boomers[40] had arrived. More has been written about the cohort born between 1946 and 1964, when birth rates spiked, than any other. First seen as firebrands and hippies, they were known as the 'flower children' who fought for racial justice in the civil rights movement, gender equality in the women's movement and lesbian and gay rights at Stonewall. In Britain, boomers were the first to be born in a free NHS hospital and the first to own homes, electronics and holidays – to some, they'd 'never had it so good'.[41] Defined by Woodstock, Beatlemania and the Vietnam War, they grew up in the suburbs with rock and roll, transistor radios, and hula hoops. They turned on, tuned in and dropped out[42] in their youth, but by the time they'd lived through the assassination of JFK, walking on the moon and Watergate, their '60s idealism gave way to '80s yuppiedom. Soon, the wearing of an Armani suit and the driving of a Porsche became top priority; rather than fighting the establishment, they became it. Indeed, it is their rampant materialism that has contributed to the world's mountain of over £3.5 trillion worth of idle assets[43] – from cars to clothing. Arguably, this boom in hyper consumption and the resulting global economic crisis led to the very birth of the Sharing Economy itself.

But as boomers reach retirement and their racking up of debt causes personal suffering, they are turning to the Sharing Economy to make some cash. Indeed, 28% of those aged 55 and older have already used a Sharing Economy service.[44] This generation needs to share and, as empty nesters, they're well equipped. It's often the boomers who own the assets and they're becoming more reliant on income from online Sharing platforms than their younger counterparts.[45] Now, they're the fastest growing group to participate, answering an increasing demand for access to shared assets with a quarter of those aged 55 and older as providers in the sector and 16% being over 65.[46]

The value boomers place on relationships and the speed at which they have adopted technology as productivity tools chimes well with the Sharing trend. Social Sharing is also popular with boomers, who share more content on Facebook than any other generation.[47]

It is well documented that ageing is becoming one of the most important social issues of the 21st century; the Sharing Economy then, could be our greatest hope. The latest trend is 'gradual retirement', with the over 60s using the gig economy as a transition, a way to work and live at the same time. Of course, it isn't for everyone; not all boomers are suited to this entrepreneurial, non-traditional, live-work-life, without the trappings and benefits of conventional employment. But for those who are, it's proving fruitful. Gig platform Fiverr has seen the growth in vendors aged 55–64 increase 375% and pet Sharing platform PetCloud saw boomers earning five times more income than their millennial equivalents.[48] Notably, 41% of senior hosts reported that the extra income allows them to stay in their homes longer.[49]

We've seen the advent of caring, Sharing services like Room2Care, a Miami based care service for elders, while in the Netherlands, Oma's Pop-Up uses temporary restaurants to reintegrate isolated senior citizens. In the UK, TrustonTap connects self-employed care workers with older people who want to live at home independently. Private social care group Cera, which matches carers with elders, partnered with Barts Health NHS Trust to look after elderly patients once they leave hospital, and their partnership with taxi app Gett uses drivers to courier non-prescription medication from chemists to homes.

Baby boomers may have failed to realise the ideals of their youth, but the Sharing Economy is an opportunity to do just that. The silver Sharers have the ability to use their life lessons, combining the Sharing values and experiences of their youth (the desire for justice, equality, dismantling the status quo) alongside their ability to work hard and get things done. Boomers may be the last cohort to join the Sharing Economy, but they stand to gain the most and it is they who will grow it.

SHARING TIME: BRIGHTON & HOVE SEAFRONT, UK.

# THE DIGITAL BOOMER

**Phyllis Santamaria** is 73 years old and was born in Texas, USA. She founded social enterprise *Microfinance Without Borders* and currently runs *Learning Without Borders*. Phyllis has embraced technology throughout her life as a means to share resources.

"At Learning Without Borders, we're working on a platform for increasing access to employment for people with disabilities. We give communities access to create a future worth living and we've developed a model called 3.0, based on the internet. So, 1.0, when the internet started, we would just receive information; 2.0 was when we could start interacting (e.g. Facebook); 3.0 is where you have a platform and can create a Sharing enterprise such as BlaBlaCar. A 1.0 company is mainly profit-centric, a 2.0 company is people centric and 3.0 is purpose-centric. We want people to have fulfilment in their work because we spend so much of our lives working and get joy from fulfilling our purpose.

I was brought up in the segregated south and my parents had the equivalent of Airbnb a long time ago; my grandmother had four rooming houses and they earned money by having people stay. I'm from a very large family, I have nine brothers and sisters and I'm the eldest daughter. Unusually for that time, because it was the segregated south, black people, African Americans, lived with us and there was one man named Andrew who worked as a porter in the supermarket up the street and he would wheel home a trolley full of day-old goods and vegetables that they couldn't sell at the supermarket. I remember as a child, looking up to him and saying, 'Mr Andrew, why are you doing this for us?' and he said, 'Well, Mr Foley (that was my father's name) has a lot of mouths to feed,' and that made a really big impression on me as a child … (she cries) and … (cries) … that's why I'm really committed to social justice, because he was killed by white people and they never got punished for his murder (cries).

I'm atypical for my generation, in the 1980s I was into computers in a big way and we were linking multi-media. People say to me, 'Wow, you're like a millennial with your technology!' I use social media when I'm going to events so that people who aren't fortunate enough to be there can participate online. For some segments of my generation, technology has had a huge impact, for others they'll use it in their washing machine where they don't realise it's there, but it hasn't had the same impact. I think sharing cuts across generations, I don't think it's a generational thing. I'm a proponent of the Sharing Economy and I'm a baby boomer. I think the early adopters are a certain segment of each generation."

PHYLLIS SANTAMARIA AT HOME, CENTRAL LONDON, UK.

# THE LIFELONG SHARER

" My generation was brought up after the war when there was rationing, so we didn't have that many things. What people spend on Christmas and birthdays today is extraordinary. There's been a shift now to electronic, virtual things. Kids live on iPads, you don't have toys anymore, you have games for your iPad and sharing becomes different when you don't have things. Consumption patterns are different, but the sharing motive is a more ethical, religious thing, it's the way you are and I'm not sure that's changed at all. "

**Michael Norton, OBE, director, Centre for Innovation in Voluntary Action**

MICHAEL NORTON OBE, (75) DIRECTOR OF THE CENTRE FOR INNOVATION IN VOLUNTARY ACTION (CIVA) AND AUTHOR OF 365 WAYS TO CHANGE THE WORLD, AT HOME, HAMPSTEAD, LONDON, UK.

# THE SENIOR CO-HOUSERS

Anna Watkins (64), Helen Matcham (78) and Sheila Nicolson (80) are founding members of *OWCH, Older Women's Co-Housing*. They have created their own community for women over the age of 50, in a new purpose-built block of flats in High Barnet, London, called New Ground.

**Anna:** Co-housing is where everybody has their own flat, but you have some common areas, like a kitchen, a dining room and some meals are shared. We make decisions through consensus. It's called an 'intentional community'. We knew each other when we moved in and we are signed up to be good neighbours. I watched my mother die in her terraced house, happy with the relationships she had with her neighbours. I asked her if she had good neighbours, she said, 'They're wonderful' and I said, 'What do they do for you?' She said, 'That man opposite waves at me.' I thought, I don't want to be waved at, I want conversation, a cup of tea, a glass of wine, I want more than waving. So, I went online, and found a co-housing community.

**Sheila:** My friends who've come to visit see the appeal of co-housing. They are private people who would not consider being outside a unit of a marriage, but I could see one friend thinking, 'Well, my husband could die, then this could be for me.'

**Anna:** Here, nobody will slam their door in your face, we care about each other not for each other, so someone can't just park their mother here and say, 'The community will take care of her.' It's important that there is a public and a private space, so if you don't feel like sharing your time, smiles or cups of tea, you don't have to, but then when you do feel like it, you can be part of the community.

**Helen:** In the world of work, we've all had to cooperate before and in a way, it's doing it for your own benefit rather than the workplace.

**Sheila:** As you get older it's important to have sharing built in, because I never thought ageing would be difficult but it is. If you start young doing this kind of sharing, the world's going to be a better place, because you learn cooperation. It could put an end to a lot of the negatives that we live with in our lives, because when you are supported, you are a much more positive person.

**Anna:** If co-housing really took off, older people could have a better life and be less of a drain on our limited resources. We could heal each other in an encouraging, living well way, where you have a lot of people cheering you on. There is a time bomb of old people being lonely. Old age is scary. Senior co-housing is almost like a comfortable sweater to wear, but it's a human sweater.

SHARING A LAUGH: (L TO R) ANNA WATKINS, SHEILA NICOLSON, HELEN MATCHAM; ANNA'S HANDS; COMMUNAL BOOKS IN COSY CORNER; THE GARDEN, NEW GROUND CO-LIVING, HIGH BARNET, LONDON, UK.

TEN AGES OF SHARING: MARINE DRIVE, MUMBAI, INDIA.

# TEN AGES OF SHARING

**Inder Bhatia** is 86 years old and was born in Pakistan. He was a refugee who migrated to Mumbai at the time of the India–Pakistan partition in 1947. He's an ardent believer in knowledge sharing, has a particular theory of sharing and blogs on the topic.

**" A person's attitude to sharing varies with age, it changes every decade. I believe there are ten ages of sharing.**

When you are 0–10, you are a child, you share with your parents, the sharing is unequal because you are a dependent. From 10–20, you share with friends and the sharing becomes reciprocal. Age 20–30 is when romantic relationships become important and you share with your spouse or partner. If you didn't receive affection as a child, or have friends at school, you may become more solitary and sharing can feel difficult. Thirty to 40 is when, if you have found a caring, sharing relationship in your 20s, you become happy. It's also when your own children may enter your life and you share with them. Between 40 to 50, people focus on earning money. This stage is about sharing with your career and being selfish. You try to amass money for yourself, corruption tends to happen amongst this age group. This stage of sharing is based on fear, 'I've done all this sharing but what about my future?'

From 50 onwards, you share with people you don't know, if you have the money, you will travel and see the world. You realise at this age that we are all human and you can connect and share with strangers. Often, there is more sharing at this age. Sixty to 70 is the age of utility, so you need to make yourself useful. How much you can share depends on the skills you have. Between 70 and 80, if you are healthy and able to enjoy life, then you are more likely to share. At this age, we try to be friends with doctors! If you are ill and feel more depressed, you spend time focusing on your own illnesses, rather than sharing with others.

Ah! Eighty to 90, this is the decade I'm working on! It's the age of sharing when you have no responsibilities, others share with you, you can receive help and support and if you are well, you can share with those less fortunate. Then there's 90–100, when your sharing depends on how active you are at this stage! I'm not there yet! **"**

A LIFE WORTH SHARING: INDER BHATIA AT HOME, MUMBAI, INDIA.

"Today I've had an opportunity to share my story with you, I've enjoyed that. You reminded me of my past and of the different ages of sharing. For me, sharing this knowledge is the best way I can help others."

**Inder Bhatia**

PRIDE 2018, BRIGHTON AND HOVE, UK.

# SHARING
# BY GENDER

In 2017, Canada issued the world's first health card for a baby that does not state the child's sex. Requested by non-binary, transgender parent, Kori Doty, who identifies as neither male nor female, the British Columbian ID carries a 'U' in the box where a child's sex is 'normally' specified. But when it comes to gender and our interpretation of it today, what exactly is 'normal'? Yes, gender is certainly the topic of the decade. The sheer mention of the word that originated from the Old French 'gendre' or 'type' and the Latin 'genus' meaning 'birth, family or nation' is likely to ignite multifarious opinions, wherever and whenever it is raised. We are living in an era of economic, social and environmental flux, witnessing an increased societal consciousness of the need for justice, fairness and the rejection of previously accepted norms. Sharing is at the heart of these shifts and is not just about tangible asset sharing, but offers a redefinition of 'other', a sharing of power and an understanding that what has previously dominated won't do so for much longer.

2018 marked 100 years since women in the UK first got the vote, yet we are still subjected to sexism, violence and are vastly underrepresented in the political realm worldwide. The unacceptable statistics speak for themselves – each minute, 28 girls are married before they are ready[50] and up to 35% of women today have experienced sexual or physical violence.[51] The gender pay gap knows no borders; whether you're a farmer in Nigeria, or Jennifer Lawrence in Hollywood, it's likely you'll only be paid two-thirds as much as your male equivalent.

But something is shifting. From #MeToo[52] to the Time's Up campaign,[53] women have had enough. We're witnessing the emergence of a Sharing system based on fairness, mutual respect and caring. Often cited as a strong attribute of femininity, though some would say that is a stereotype too, sharing is indissolubly linked with caring, a quality that is being applied to create new systems that empower all genders rather than maintain the patriarchal status quo. In the past five years, we've seen a proliferation of initiatives enabling women to share everything from cars to cash. There's Present, an app that connects women and the causes they care about, HeraHub, offering shared workspaces, and Piya Bose's Girls on the Go Club, where women take shared expeditions to inspire world change.

From CityGirl to the ubiquitous Mumsnet, the Sharing universe owes much to women. Issues such as online safety and digital identity have come to the fore. The Sharing Economy has been quick to respond with new trust apps, verifying identities, facial recognition tools and background checks. The prominence of ratings and reviews has resulted in a world where digital reputation is everything, trust is the secret of the Sharing Economy – first we trust, then we share.[54] This newfound trust has sparked ride-sharing aps exclusively for women from Indonesia's Ojesy, a motorbike sharing service for Muslim women, to LA-based HopSkipDrive, created by mums who provide a ride service for kids with a pool of 'Caredrivers'. Not surprising then that, as consumers, women's participation in the Sharing Economy is increasing with a 65% take up.[55]

Crowdfunding is another Sharing win for women. Women are five times more successful at raising money via crowdfunding sites than traditional venture capital routes,[56] they raise more money than men,[57] and are more likely to attract 'activist' female backers who fund women in under-represented industries. This women-helping-women trend is removing the male gatekeepers to currency, democratising and making entrepreneurship more socially responsible. Research shows that women are more likely to make business decisions based on ethics rather than profit,[58] 40% of social enterprises (Sharing businesses) are led by women,[59] and women are more likely to pay fair wages, employ people from disadvantaged backgrounds and create value collaboratively.[60]

Much has been said about the supposed shortcomings of the 'gig economy'. But what's wildly misunderstood is that gig work (not suited to everyone) often provides opportunities for those of all genders who have been pushed to the margins of the labour market. Freelancer Union's Sara Horowitz believes 'freelancing is feminist', since most full-time freelancers are women. But women aren't alone; frustrated with the gender pay gap, discrimination and lack of opportunities in the male-dominated corporate world, transgendered, non-binary and people of all genders are choosing the gig economy as a way to achieve financial independence.

In the gender equality stakes, the Sharing Economy is making headway in every area, from the home to the workplace and, ultimately, women's contribution to the economy and society at large. Of course, gender parity will only happen when all of us share power, whatever our gender.

# THE EQUALITY SHARER

**Nanjira Sambuli is a 29-year-old intrapreneur from Kenya and campaigns for fair internet access. She is the Digital Equality Advocacy Manager at the *Worldwide Web Foundation*, established by Sir Tim Berners-Lee, the inventor of the internet.**

" Anyone, anywhere, regardless of their age, the geography they're in or their gender, should be able to exercise their choice to connect or disconnect from the internet. I focus on women's rights online, trying to make sure that the web remains a safe space for women, especially those in the developing world who are left offline because of economic inequalities and may not have the disposable income to buy the devices that get them connected. I come from a part of the world where, if I want to go to another country, there are all sorts of physical barriers, including the cost of travel. But the web made that possible. The web can help people who have been left behind due to discrimination or bias and can make them feel more comfortable because they know that they are not alone and, if they are harassed, there's a recourse mechanism they can take.

Sometimes when we talk about sharing, it's tangible stuff, we never talk about the softer stuff – your time, your energy, that idea of always showing up and being present. There's still that inequality. I can go into a room of men and be the only black woman and I have to keep showing up because, unless I do, one day that door is going to be locked. Even if you are the person for the diversity poster, if you are in a room and everybody looks the same and they're making decisions about the world, it's a problem. So keeping on showing up, have a voice.

People joke that if Mark Zuckerberg came from Africa, he would never have made it, because a kid who has ideas but doesn't have access to the store, it's like they've been punished by being born on the wrong side of the tracks.

It would be tragic if the Sharing Economy just benefits white men. If the narrative is beautiful but the economy itself is still running the same old school way. Ideally, in terms of gender equality, the Sharing Economy would be a game-changer. If, now, you're forced to focus on surviving but Sharing helps you to reclaim the systems that allow you to thrive then it could change the way politics and development is done. If the Sharing Economy posits itself as a survival thing, then people could jump on it much quicker. "

---

DIGITAL EQUALITY CAMPAIGNER, NANJIRA SAMBULI FROM KENYA, AFRICA.

# THE SUPERMARKET SHARERS

Ruth Anslow (42), sister Amy (39) and Jack Simmonds (33) are the Founders of *HISBE*, a social enterprise supermarket, based on Sharing, community and sustainable principles. I spoke to Ruth about how *HISBE* came to be.

" We've built an alternative supermarket model through collaboration and caring. We got fed up with the way supermarkets do business, it has a negative effect on people, communities and local economies – it's the opposite of sharing. We're about keeping profits in communities and in the hands of the producers. Our big vision is to transform the food industry by reinventing the way supermarkets do business.

We are called HISBE, which stands for How It Should Be. We started with a set of values and a vision of how a supermarket should be. We created a sourcing policy that would contribute to a fairer, more ethical food industry. We consider sharing in many aspects of what we do, from the way we source and present products, the range, which we build through collaboration with customers and how we are funded through crowdfunding. This business exists because hundreds of people have helped us build it.

We help a lot of small suppliers get going, we share the profit with them, out of every pound that gets spent in HISBE, 68p goes to suppliers. The equivalent figure in supermarkets is 9p. If they're given the right price and conditions, they can make the products that contribute to a better food system. At the tills, you can see a pie chart breakdown of how much money has gone to the supplier, store, staff bills and how much profit we make.

We deliberately undercharge on many areas of the shop, because by testing an offer that hits the average income level, we are going to make the stuff mainstream. So we collaborate with our customers because their purchasing power is what creates the industry. They're voting for our sausages, not Sainsbury's.

My gender is irrelevant to what I do; it's about values, dreams and purpose rather than gender. But I worked in big corporates for 15 years and they were male dominated. I saw the values were more about money and more male; certainly all of the senior people were male and you had to be like them to succeed. I want people to copy this business. Tomorrow, if Tesco copied us, we could go home, because the food industry would be transformed. I love the idea that people would look at me as a social entrepreneur and copy my approach to business. I want to be a role model for men and women equally. I see myself as a world-class entrepreneur and I don't make the distinction of gender. "

HOW IT SHOULD BE: (L TO R) RUTH AND AMY ANSLOW, HISBE SUPERMARKET, BRIGHTON, UK.

**bioD**

# 100%

**MADE IN BRITAIN, BY US.**

Every one of our product boxes, sprays, hand pumps and bottles contains 100% of our very own product, which is all made in our factory in the UK, by us and no one else.

**NATURAL PLANT-BASED INGREDIENTS.**

We only use ingredients that are naturally derived or plant based. They have all come from an ethical, sustainable source.

**OF OUR RANGE IS HYPOALLERGENIC.**

All of the products we manufacture are hypo-allergenic, which means they are much kinder to those with sensitive skin. We are the only producer that offers this through

**WE LEAVE OUT ALL THE HORRIBLE STUFF.**

Using only natural ingredients means that our products biodegrade faster than the EU standard requirement — no need to use 97%

# THE SHARING GRANDMA

Alia Dasouqi is a 61-year-old Muslim from Jaffa, Israel. She cooks 'Arabian Nights' dinners in her home three times a week for 20 people via the Sharing platform *EatWith*.

❝ I started hosting dinners because my kids grew up and left home and I had free time. I went to a meeting in the Jaffa community and heard about a project called EatWith. They asked who could host dinners at home. With the family's support, I decided to try it.

It's interesting meeting new people, telling them about my family, living in Israel and in Jaffa particularly. It's important to me to tell people how Jews and Arabs live together and what life is really like when you live here. At first it was hard to let strangers into my house, but from the first dinner, it felt good to share my home and I saw that they were good people. On EatWith, you can see the names of those who have booked and what they do for a living. Over time, I've built up trust.

I was not very confident before I started sharing and opening up my home. In traditional Arab society, wives are supposed to cook and raise the kids, that's your place in life. I wasn't a speaker. I was a silent wife. Times are changing for Arab women; my daughters and grandchildren (I have eight!) have grown up differently to me.

**Hosting shared dinners has really empowered me. It has given me a stage, a place to talk. Previously, I only cooked for my family and it is not appreciated in the same way because you do it every day. When people from around the world come to the dinners, taste the food and say, 'WOW! Your food is amazing', you start to appreciate yourself.**

My culinary skills have been recognised and now I am considered an important chef in the Arab community and I have had the opportunity to cook with very famous chefs in Israel. My signature dish is called Maqloobeh, an upside-down savoury aubergine cake. It looks like a cake, but it's not a dessert, you turn it over and eat it, it's looks beautiful and people love it! ❞

ALIA DASOUQI HOSTING HER ARABIAN SUPPER CLUB, JAFFA, ISRAEL.

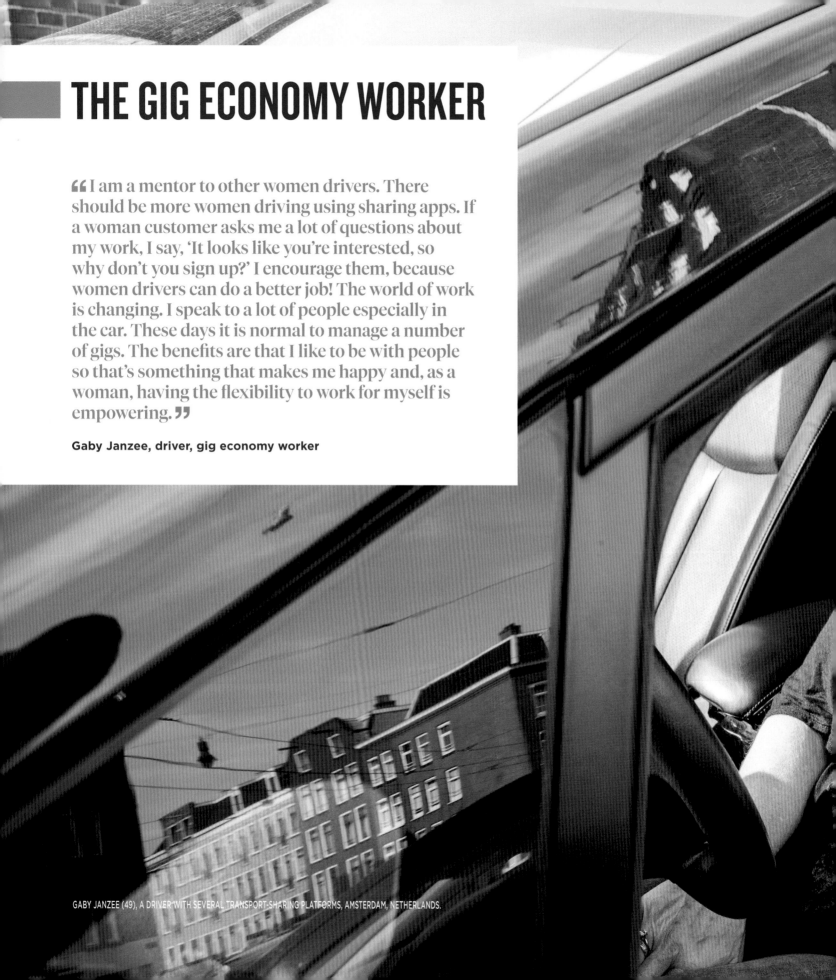

# THE GIG ECONOMY WORKER

❝I am a mentor to other women drivers. There should be more women driving using sharing apps. If a woman customer asks me a lot of questions about my work, I say, 'It looks like you're interested, so why don't you sign up?' I encourage them, because women drivers can do a better job! The world of work is changing. I speak to a lot of people especially in the car. These days it is normal to manage a number of gigs. The benefits are that I like to be with people so that's something that makes me happy and, as a woman, having the flexibility to work for myself is empowering.❞

**Gaby Janzee, driver, gig economy worker**

GABY JANZEE (49), A DRIVER WITH SEVERAL TRANSPORT-SHARING PLATFORMS, AMSTERDAM, NETHERLANDS.

# THE IDENTITY SHARER

**Iman Bibars** is 57 years old and from Egypt. She created the first micro-credit programme in the Arab world, to upskill women and provide them with ID cards.

" Wanting to change the world was not common in Egyptian culture. I went into the poorest areas, where the women 'waste pickers' were collecting garbage. I wanted to work with them as they have nothing. If their husband dies, leaves them, or disappears, they either have to get remarried or become a prostitute and the kids become destitute. They have no choice. I wanted to help them have a choice.

In 1984, I started the first micro-credit programme in the Arab world. Previously, if you were setting up a micro-credit program, a man had to be the guarantor. We didn't want women to depend on men, we wanted women to guarantee each other. People said, 'Women will not be able to repay the loans; they have no ID cards.' So for the first ten years, we gave micro-credit with no guarantee, no down payment and the women did not have to be literate. Every single woman paid us back.

Not having an identity card means these women don't legally exist. They come from rural areas, they don't go to school, they're not registered with the government, they get married under age, are put on their husband's ID, he leaves and she no longer exists. Eighty per cent of women in slum areas at that time did not have ID. It took us a long time to find out how to get ID for someone who doesn't have ID. We demonstrated that women are credible. In comparison to men, 99% of women repay, whereas 80% of men don't pay back.

Now, 97% of women in the country have ID. This kind of sharing changed their lives. We gave women the opportunity not to marry the guy who's going to kick their kids or not become a sex worker, that's empowering. Now women can become an owner of a supermarket, they do not have to die of poverty, sell their kids or their kidneys.

Gender is about power relations. As women, we have participated in a 9 to 5 work ecosystem; in reality that's a male thing. So women have to compete with them with their rules. Women have shared but men haven't. We talk about reproductive rights; I say, we are reproducing the community, the armies, the ministers and the government. Pregnancy and taking care of kids should be a public not a private matter.

We work twice as hard to achieve anything as women. Even in the West we don't get the same salaries as men. Sharing is the only way to empower vulnerable groups. What's needed is equal sharing from both genders, which has not happened up to now; women are better at sharing than men. "

WOMAN OF EMPOWERMENT: IMAN BIBARS FROM EGYPT.

# THE POWER SHARER

**Servane Mouazan is 43 years old and from France. She is the founder of *Ogunte*, a social enterprise that helps female social entrepreneurs make a positive impact on people and planet.**

"Sharing is something that is not easy to practise. It's a skill that you aspire to use, I try to practise that in my work. 'Ogunte' means female spirit. I support and amplify women in social enterprises, because if women had more opportunities and were less subject to gender inequalities, they could bring more to the economy, to life and the world would be better off. We work on how they can make better use of their resources, their sustainability and viability, how they use finance and create positive impact. We work on learning, growth of confidence, not just how bold they can be in fundraising, but encouraging people to dare to share their stories, skills and to ask for help when needed.

There are different definitions for power. I like the definition of power as energy, like fuel, renewable energy, the kind that makes you 'go'. I use it on our tagline 'A better world powered by women'. It's not a hierarchical, top-down power, it's power-energised fuel, inspired by women. You can use this energy for each other's good. Energy flows, you can't store it indefinitely; it's fluid, it has to bounce back, it goes through other materials, this is where the sharing happens.

Sharing is not a fluffy thing, there's something bold, it's a decision. Understand sharing as one of the parts of the economy is not an easy thing to do and I'm not talking about swapping your sewing machine or your kilo of sugar against something equivalent, it's much bigger than that.

If women are not paid for the time they spend supporting others, then they're not taken seriously. It's about being clear that people are misusing the word 'sharing' in the Sharing Economy, and understanding that sharing is equally as important as a financial transaction. There's nothing inherently female about sharing. There's little difference between men and women. There's a sexual difference, but the rest of it is perpetuated myths and stereotypes that put people in corners. Because we engage in these stereotypes, for some people it becomes a reality. Because of these acquired behaviours, then we tend to see women as more communal and men as more individual, or exclusive, but you can disrupt that.

Sharing shouldn't be gendered. Sharing is an act of boldness and leadership, it's a choice, it's decision-making, it doesn't belong more to women than men. "

OGUNTE FOUNDER, SERVANE MOUAZAN FROM FRANCE.

# THE GENDER CHALLENGER

**Asmaa Guedira** is 31 years old and from Morocco. She runs a Sharing project called *Hyper-Gender* which challenges gender stereotypes in new economy communities.

"Sharing is rooted in my DNA. I grew up in Morocco, in a liberal family, sharing everything. My dad was a feminist; I was told I could do whatever I wanted. Entering the professional world, I realised how much gender bias existed. I was dating a girl, so I felt alienated in this environment. Immersing myself in the sharing economy, I realised no one was judging me but I recognised the need to address gender issues and stereotypes. 'Hyper-Gender' is about the paradigm shift happening in gender, especially in new communities that revamp and call themselves 'sharing economy', but are no different in reality.

You cannot have toxic masculinity in an environment where you promote sharing, trust and openness. My goal is to bring different people together without labels. The idea is to be free to explore, express and question your gender, identity and sexuality.

Transgender and non-binary is a big topic in the UK and US. People are questioning this masculine–feminine binary. I don't align with this new movement of transgender and non-binary, because I don't want to create a label that again excludes others. This whole life of being a collaborative activist reconciled me with men because I met men that questioned the machismo I always hated. In these new economy communities, I saw men rejecting the aggression, competition and toxic masculinity that is ruining the world.

We see challenges for women in these new economies. Uber is not the Sharing Economy yet it's considered part of it. These on-demand ride-sharing services are mostly used by women, especially in developing countries where mobility is an issue. I hate this company Uber, because the values are definitely not based on sharing, but when I travel to Egypt, Lebanon or Morocco and even in Paris, I download it, because it's the safest tool. There's a challenge to build new Sharing tools, from a company that has sharing values and offers safety solutions for all genders.

What the Sharing Economy does for women is to deconstruct barriers. If you look at the traditional economy, the Sharing Economy is more inclusive. There's space for us all, whatever gender we identify with, to grow and adopt these values. With the connections and networks that the internet allows, through social media, through this kind of dialogue, I see opportunities for this culture shift to happen. It gives me a lot of excitement and hope."

ASMAA GUEDIRA, FOUNDER OF HYPER-GENDER, FROM MOROCCO.

# THE VOLUNTEER

**Claire Green** is 51 years old and from the UK. A transgender woman, Claire collects spare toiletries and goods for homeless people and volunteers for the charity, *Crisis*.

"I give out packages of shampoos, soaps, toothpaste and sanitary towels to homeless people. I'm conscious of not giving money, but time, and engaging with people. Sometimes they offload problems, it gives them the opportunity to talk. I try and do that as often as I can; it culminates at Christmas when I volunteer at Crisis in Kings Cross.

I've seen a lot of homeless people on my travels up and down the country. I've had conversations with people who've been robbed, lost their job, or a relationship had broken down and they've slipped through the safety net that we think is there, but in reality isn't. There are reasons for homelessness. It made me realise it's a big problem and in the last four years it's doubled. I felt I needed to do more.

The majority of the time they're on the street, they're dirty and they struggle to get places where they can wash and go to the toilet, so I started collecting toiletries that I would pick up in hotels. There's this mountain of unused toiletries and if you use them once, the hotels are going to throw them away, so you can give them out again. It's less waste and they're going to people who need them.

With the loyalty cards you get from coffee shops, you get a free coffee with every six, so I share those too. I encourage my friends to bring their spare toiletries and share them. Now they're getting involved and it feels like I'm a conduit. I've been in positions where I've been down and out of luck and I've had help. It's repaying the help that's been shown to me. I try to make one person's day a bit better. If I can do that once a day, for someone, then it makes me feel I'm not putting my head down and walking past.

On my first day volunteering, I had a cry in the toilets because the stories you hear aren't nice, but then you realise that's why you are doing it. I see that 90% of the homeless are men on the streets. With the volunteers it's 60–40 women. Perhaps there are so many men on the streets because it's the stubbornness of not wanting to seek help, not sharing when things go wrong.

It's good for people of all genders to be seen sharing. We seem to be in such a rush to do everything, sometimes it's hard to remember to take the time to help someone. Regardless of gender, if you share kindness, that's the main thing. Volunteering shows others they matter, that they're not being ignored."

CLAIRE GREEN, TRAFALGAR STREET, BRIGHTON, UK.

# THE MENTOR AND MENTEE

**Anj Handa** is 42 and from Leeds in the UK. She is the founder of *Inspiring Women Changemakers.* She mentors and enables women to lead transformational change in society.

**Ashley North** is 32 years old and from Barnsley in the UK. She has been mentored by Anj Handa for three years.

**" Anj:** I mentor women who are leading social change at work, in business, in their communities and the world. I've seen the power of sharing by teaching women how to speak up for themselves. Mentoring has helped to propel them forward, it's a form of sharing, it builds change-makers of the future. All my mentees are now in a place of strength where they feel empowered and in turn will mentor others, creating a more resilient society.

**Ashley:** A lot of my life has been abuse and trauma and, before I met Anj, I carried this stuff around with me. Mentoring is true sharing, it's helped me to let go of shame, to learn to be my full self. Everyone goes through struggles and most of the time people hide this away because they think they are dealing with stuff on their own.

**Anj:** Mentoring is so two-way because I've got things from my mentees that they've reflected back to me and that's sharing. You don't give to get, but it's a by-product.

**Ashley:** It should be a normal experience to be able to share your story with no judgement.

**Anj:** A lot of men don't share their emotions because they're worried about being seen as weak. Older men struggle, because they say what's my place? Younger men can be more open and giving, so some of it's generational. If we had a sharing economy, women could participate fully, they'd be empowered through education and job opportunities.

**Ashley:** The reason a lot of people of any gender struggle with addiction is because they want to be numb, but if you are given a safe space to share these things, to feel them, they can leave you, you can feel empowered to pass that on and share it; there's the ripple of it. **"**

YOU'LL NEVER WALK ALONE: (L TO R) ANJ HANDA AND ASHLEY NORTH, ROUNDHAY PARK, LEEDS, UK.

"Being mentored has shown me that sharing means allowing people to see the whole of you, not just the parts you think look good. Sharing is like allowing there to be a mirror, so people can see reflections of themselves and see both the good and the things they need work on."

**Ashley North, mentee**

"Online identity and trust are the biggest challenges in the Sharing Economy. Safety is a bigger issue for women and some Sharing Economy platforms enable you to request 'women only'. For women, the Sharing Economy is offering a safer, more trusted access to services that are tracked online. So we have more information about who requested which service, at what time, in what location and who they were meeting. Previously, we didn't have ratings and reviews, or ways of verifying others. It's much harder now to do something dishonest without that affecting your online reputation. There are a few 'fake reviews' but you can compare and see what the majority believe. The group have more power than the individual fake review."

# THE HEALTHY SHARER

**Emilie Jacquetton is 38 years old and was born in France. She is the founder of Sharing platform *Ouiwin*, a wellbeing marketplace to enable people to cope with their health challenges.**

" When you experience illness, you have so much information to share, so I want to develop a way that people can easily share those health experiences. Imagine being in a bar, where there is a group meeting to discuss issues around Alzheimer's. There would be a professional, someone from the Alzheimer's Association and family members who are dealing with the disease. I want to do this in an open way where people can share in a safe, supportive and social environment, not just a sterile medicalised one. It's not just about group events; people can meet one-to-one. I want to help people become more informed about their healthcare needs. My goal is to bring quality information through reviews and greater efficiencies for doctors, so instead of just having your 10-minute appointment, there are longer group sessions where you can get more information.

I believe I can be part of changing the way healthcare is organised and delivered by using a Sharing Economy approach. There is already a trend of 'patient experts' – I want people to be part of their own healthcare ecosystem.

We need to convince more people to try more platforms because the volume will be the force behind the Sharing Economy that will make it safer for all genders. An expert from one of the health associations I work with, explained the power of the group model. She said, 'From the group comes the magic.' I believe the same is true for the Sharing Economy. From the group of people that you never imagined knowing before comes the magic. "

EMILIE JACQUETTON, AVINGUDA DIAGONAL, BARCELONA, SPAIN.

# THE ON-DEMAND SHARER

66 Sharing is an incredible improvement in efficiency. Through on-demand services, it's making use of the excess quantities capitalism has created and giving them a new usage in an environmental way. Gender differences in the Sharing Economy tend to be related to the type of things you want to share. I believe Sharing platforms and technology solutions can completely balance or equalise gender and resolve gender differences, since the need for specific things can be tailored to both sides. 99

**Sebastian Steinhauser, founder, Parcelly**

SEBASTIAN STEINHAUSER (34) FROM GERMANY, FOUNDER OF LOGISTICS SHARING PLATFORM, PARCELLY (MAIN IMAGE); (TOP RIGHT) TECH HUB, LXFACTORY, LISBON; (BOTTOM LEFT) REPAIR SHOP, BARCELONA; (BOTTOM RIGHT) COFFEE COMPANY, WATERLOOPLEIN MARKET, AMSTERDAM.

# SHARING PASSIONS

**David Bramwell** is 49 years old and from Doncaster in the UK. In 2004, he founded the *Catalyst Club*, a monthly Brighton event that plays tribute to the traditions of French Salons and debating societies. It's a place where everyday folk share their passions, however bizarre.

"I came out of a long-term relationship, having been replaced by someone who was 'younger, but more mature'. I had a thing to learn about sharing, so I took myself off to visit different sharing communities. It made me want to bring community and sharing into my neighbourhood, so I set up the Catalyst Club. There is an open platform for three guest speakers to share anything that they are passionate about. People are often afraid of public speaking, but this night shows we are all capable of telling good stories and sharing our knowledge. It's courage, facing fears and sharing causes to the wider world. We did a programme with Radio 4 about public speaking. I sent an email to find a guinea pig who was terrified of public speaking. I worked with Claire and we chose 'desiccated animal turds' as a topic, because it's Brighton, and she had a collection of them in her house. I told her to throw her notes away, she knew her stuff. She got the courage to be the final speaker on a night where we had an interview with the head of TED. Claire came up and nailed it.

The audience don't know the topics, because it prevents prejudice, it's about the people not the subjects. My favourite was a bum reading talk from a Japanese performance artist. There are only three bum readers in the world – rumpologists they're called between the three of them, they read the bottom like a palm reader reads a palm. Sylvester Stallone's mother is number one in the world! People share something that's unique to them.

In terms of gender differences, at the Catalyst Club, (I have to be careful what I say) men may have a slight tendency to share facts and information in a more straightforward way and women's stories could be more emotionally based, but these might be societal and cultural – I don't know if we do see things differently. I've worked on the ratio of male to female speakers. When we started it was two men to one woman. Last year we had 19 male speakers, 17 female, 3 transgender and non-binary.

As far as I know this is the only egalitarian night. It's a live, old-fashioned sharing of knowledge that's spontaneous. I love doing it. I'm as excited 14 years on as I was when I first started because I don't know which way it's going to turn, it always keeps me on my toes."

(LTO R) DAVID BRAMWELL, JONATHAN NEWMAN AND ALEXANDRA LOSKE, CATALYST CLUB, LATEST MUSIC BAR, BRIGHTON, UK.

# THE ROLE MODEL

**Haitham Deeb** is a 30-year-old Palestinian. He is a farmer, a football player for the Palestinian team *Jabal Al Mukaber* and a teacher at the *Ahmad Sameh Peace School* in East Jerusalem. Haitham acts as a role model for students, sharing opportunities and showing that an alternative to violence is possible.

**❝ I have always believed that happiness is not so much in having as sharing. We make a living by what we get, but we make a life by what we share. Every day, no matter what I am facing, I share a smile and positive energy, because this is what the world needs.**

As a footballer, farmer and teacher, I have the opportunity to achieve what's missing in our community. I give my students the safety, love and motivation they need to accomplish their dreams in an environment where their rights are not always considered. I try to show that peace is possible, because I believe we can make this world a better place to live in. Palestinian boys love football and instead of teaching them violence and fighting, I teach them football. It's a way to communicate peacefully, an opportunity to raise our children in the right way. As a farmer, I show students how to grow flowers or trees, in the traditional Palestinian way.

**It is important for kids to grow up learning about nature, to care about their environment and to care about each other. We have a responsibility to be role models, to raise the next generation correctly, because it is they who will make a difference in the future. I do everything I can to develop a loving, caring, sharing generation.**

I met a boy in the principal's office. He had been fighting with other students and had bad grades. I worked with him, to become the role model he needed to be. I showed him the importance of education for the future of our country. Now he's getting high grades and his parents are proud of him. I develop a special relationship with every boy I teach, in order to get the best out of them and make them better men. I have to be the best that I can be, in order to make sure I am someone they would want to be. I empower them, to know that they can be like me and achieve their dreams.

Young boys and girls are the future of our world, so if we give them the best values, teach love, sharing and raise them to care about others, to have good relationships with people from different cultures and religions, we can create a less violent world where there is love and respect between nations. Through sharing, people will work harder to achieve peace and to live a safe and happy life. **❞**

PALESTINIAN HAITHAM DEEB WITH STUDENTS, AHMAD SAMEH PEACE SCHOOL, EAST JERUSALEM.

HANGING OUT AT COMMUNITISM, KARAMEIKOU 28, ATHENS, GREECE.

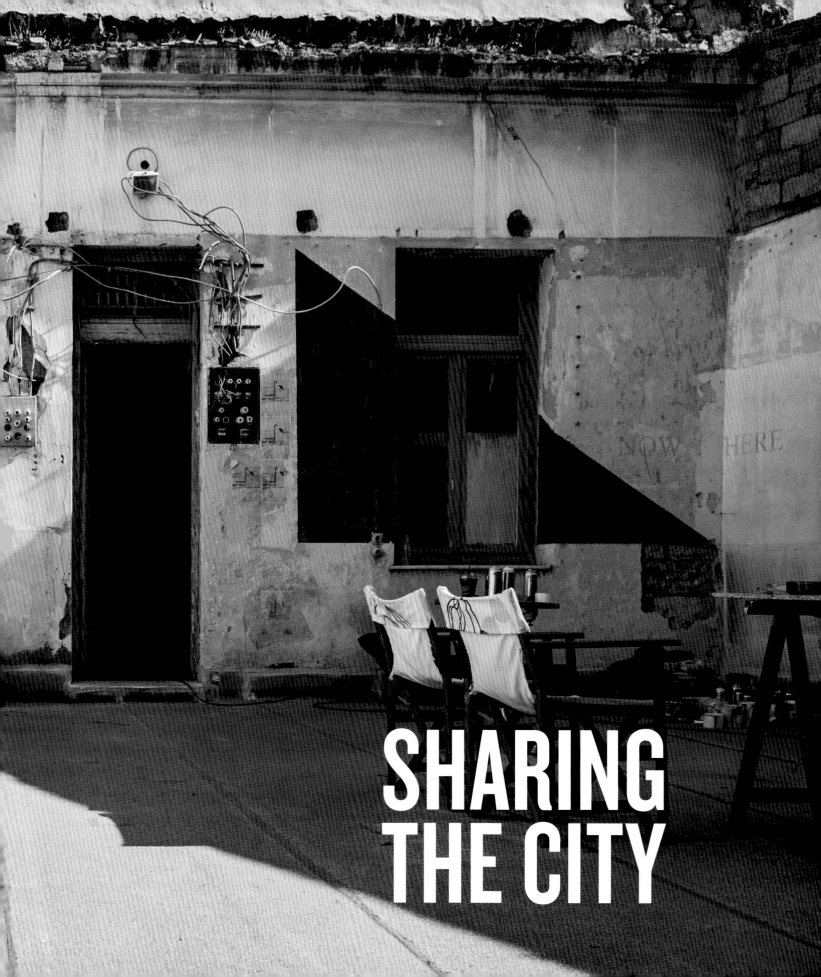

# SHARING
# THE CITY

> **" A sharing city is a playground for the Sharing Economy, everything that is needed is already there. All the cars are there, the food is there, the houses are there, you just have to divide, share and make better use of available resources within the city for everyone's benefit. "**
>
> **Harmen van Sprang, co-founder, Sharing Cities Alliance.**

That our urban environments face the considerable challenges of population, pollution and poverty is evident. But around the world, cities have another story to tell. A (not so) quiet revolution is happening. An abundance of untapped physical and human resources, combined with a desire to create sustainable eco-systems that benefit citizens, has led to the re-imagination of the city. This new approach commingles smart, networked technologies, available resources and sustainable development approaches, illustrating that when cities are co-created by the 'city-zens' themselves, we can bring everyday magic to our metropolises. Share a car and take between 9 and 13 cars off the road,[61] lower carbon and offer cheaper mobility; share the 1.3 billion tonnes of needlessly wasted food[62] and sustain those living in food poverty; create inclusive, community spaces where people can connect and watch people flourish.

Indeed, being part of a community could be life-saving. A recent three-year study in Frome, UK, showed that emergency hospital admissions fell dramatically following the introduction of a Sharing project to tackle isolation.[63] The Compassionate Frome project, launched by GP Helen Kingston, deployed health and volunteer community connectors to help patients find support. Despite a 29% increase in emergency hospital admissions across the rest of the region, in Frome, they fell by 17%. The study found that this is due in no small part to the Sharing projects catalysed by Compassionate Frome. From Men's Sheds (where men come together to make and mend), to Library of Things, where you can share and borrow needed items, the study demonstrates that there's some science to back up the notion that Sharing can save lives.

The potential for the Sharing Economy to thrive in metropolitan areas is also borne out in greater awareness[64] and higher participation rates, with residents being twice as likely to use Sharing services as their rural counterparts.[65] While cities have a great deal to gain from the Sharing Economy, more focus has been placed on the wrangling over regulation, taxation and the disruption of the status quo. We've seen services such as Airbnb banned from some cities and taxi driver protests over the introduction of car-Sharing apps. A greater understanding of the opportunity for cities is needed and an open approach that involves bringing together diverse groups to explore these possibilities. Some trailblazers are leading the way, understanding that 21st century problems need future-facing solutions.

In May 2011, Shareable, a non-profit media organisation dedicated to the Sharing transformation, co-founded by Neal Gorenflo, organised Share San Francisco. The event sparked the development of San Francisco into the world's first Sharing City and spawned a worldwide movement. Mayor Park Won-soon from Seoul, South Korea, was next, announcing in 2012 that Seoul would take up the title. Inspired by the possibilities that sharing the city could bring, from turning abandoned buildings into community repair cafés and open closets where older citizens loan formal wear to young people for interviews, to city-endorsed car Sharing, Seoul has catalysed this global movement, demonstrating the transformational power of city Sharing.[66] In this new paradigm, urban environments are becoming shared playgrounds for all, offering healthy, sustainable futures for those who live, work and breathe there.

# GREEN IN THE CITY

**Tamar Ben Shalom** is 61 years old and from Israel. She set up *Kibbutz Reshit*, a primary school and community in one of the most impoverished areas of Jerusalem, bringing the values of Sharing and nature to the city and local community.

" Sharing for me means the sharing of hope, of everything you should and could create. We came here 26 years ago, to one of the worst slum neighbourhoods in Israel. The streets were filled with garbage piles three metres high, buildings were overcrowded, generations of children were involved in drugs and gangs, and the local government referred to it as a 'deep wound' in the community.

My husband and I came from a kibbutz outside of the city; we were looking for a new challenge. It was hard for us to believe that a place like this existed, in the 1990s, in Israel, in a climate of growth. The children that were raised here knew their future was not hopeful. It was like they didn't have a sky above their heads. One of the neighbours when they saw us arriving thought we needed to open our eyes, she said, 'I have to convince you not stay here, it's not a good place to be.' She took me on a tour of the neighbourhood. I saw a lot of needles and people were throwing bags of garbage out of their windows on to the street. Then she said to me, 'Did you realise that you didn't hear a single bird sing here during this tour, not once? Even the birds left us in this forgotten place.' The woman started to cry and ran away. I was left alone with this frightening message and goosebumps all over my body.

I vowed that we would bring the birds back to this neighbourhood by building an urban kibbutz and a school for the next generation.

To achieve this, we had to work on both the physical clean-up and the societal, educational clean-up. We needed to build connections and community. Coming from a rural kibbutz background we were used to sharing everything, from material goods to money and skills. Moving to this area, we knew we would need to share in a more resilient way. By building an urban community with nature at its heart, we needed to influence not only those who lived here, but the wider community around it. We even had a local gangster from a crime syndicate visit us. He spoke about what sharing means to him. He wanted his kids to attend the school and learn the values of sharing. He recognised the importance of bringing the community together, he said 'Do you know how much energy and strength there is in unity? When we punch someone, all our fingers are tied together, we never hit anyone with our fingers apart. This urban kibbutz could show the community how unity can be used in a positive way.'

The school is based on Sharing principles. We asked all the parents from the community to share their skills, to help us build it. There was a local father working as a garbage truck driver. He was ashamed of his job, as were his kids. He told us he didn't have anything to share with us. But with garbage piled metres high, we needed someone to help us clear it, so we could turn the building into a functioning school. We asked him to bring his truck to the school. When he stood in front of 300 kids, parents and teachers, explaining how his truck worked and sharing his views on life, he was transformed. You could see his confidence growing, he realised he had something share, that he was valued. In the end he had kids surrounding the truck, wanting a demonstration, a ride and to help with the clean-up. Through sharing, he become empowered, he gained self-worth.

There were many obstacles to opening this kibbutz in the city but we achieved our mission through sharing. The whole neighbourhood has contributed. Almost every day someone comes to ask, 'How can we help?' It's a place that people really believe in, they are drawn to the positive energy here. Eventually, together, we made this place beautiful, we made it green, we showed how nature could transform the urban environment, we brought the birds back here. We demonstrated that sharing means hope. "

---

BRINGING THE BIRDS BACK: TAMAR BEN SHALOM IN THE GREENHOUSE; SCHOOLCHILDREN PLANTING SEEDLINGS; GREENHOUSE; SCHOOL MURAL, 'BLESS THE CHILDREN OF THE SCHOOL', KIBBUTZ RESHIT, JERUSALEM.

# THE SHARING CITY: AMSTERDAM

ROOFTOP VIEW OF AMSTERDAM
FROM ROCKSTART CO-WORKING.

# THE SHARING CITY DUO

Harmen van Sprang **(43)** and Pieter van de Glind **(29)** are the founders of Amsterdam-based *ShareNL* and the pioneers behind the *Sharing Cities Alliance*. The Sharing Cities Alliance is a network that connects cities worldwide and fosters city-to-city collaboration, empowering urban governments to address the Sharing Economy.

**"** **Harmen:** This mural painting translates as 'I play in the city with all that is there'. It's a great metaphor, about making better use of what already exists. The major urban challenges we face such as people living alone, or having less access to products and services, could be addressed by the Sharing Economy.

**Pieter:** A sharing city is a city that is transformed by working together with different stakeholders to open up abundance, where every citizen has access to the things they need to live a happy, connected and sustainable life. In the next two decades, three-quarters of the 9 billion people in the world will live in a city, by making efficient use of resources, enabling community sharing, we can become sustainable.

**Harmen:** When Seoul, Korea, announced that they were becoming a sharing city, we thought, Amsterdam could benefit too. We carried out some research and discovered that 84% of people here were willing to share. We saw the potential.

**Pieter:** We brought together the City Hall, the public library, insurance companies and banks, plus neighbourhood, community groups and Sharing Economy platforms. Basically, everyone that makes a city a city.

**Harmen:** It's about bringing these different groups around the table to explore, learn, make mistakes and grow from there. The city government of Amsterdam has embraced the Sharing Economy and addressed the opportunities and challenges. They were one of the first cities worldwide to agree regulation surrounding Airbnb. In 2017, we launched the Sharing Cities Alliance. Cities who sign up can access knowledge, regulations, ideas, and case studies. **"**

FOUNDERS OF THE SHARING CITIES ALLIANCE, (R TO L) HARMEN VAN SPRANG AND PIETER VAN DE GLIND BY THE SHARING CITY MURAL, AMSTERDAM, NETHERLANDS.

> **" Future cities are cities that embrace the Sharing Economy because it empowers, it's about collaboration, having citizens who are connected by technology, and by personal, social relationships. "**

**Harmen van Sprang**

# THE OFFICIAL SHARER

**Nanette Schippers** is **36 years old and is the Sharing Economy Programme Manager for the City of Amsterdam.**

"At the City of Amsterdam, we are embracing and enabling the Sharing Economy because we see a lot of opportunities. To me, a sharing city is open-minded to the developments within this new sector. It's a city that doesn't immediately say 'no' to the sharing platforms. Look into them before you ban them. I haven't met a platform yet that has said, 'No we do not want to work with the city.' Most of the time we have common goals, like preventing illegal listings; it's a question of how we can work together.

A lot of partners are involved. We definitely didn't do this by ourselves. I learnt that once you are sitting at the table with these platforms they want the same thing. They want a clean, thriving city, and they want to work together to make it beautiful. I tell people, 'Don't talk about them, talk with them and try to collaborate.'

Together, we have to determine the safest way the city and the citizens can benefit from the Sharing Economy. It is not easy to do. With the renting out of rooms (Airbnb), we didn't say 'no' immediately to people listing their homes. The city developed a policy that worked for Amsterdam, that said, 'you can rent out your home, but there are some rules', for example it is limited to 60 days a year. From there, we worked with the platforms to prevent illegal listings.

Here, we developed 'city principles'. For example, that people working for platforms have (at least) a basic income. It's about sharing knowledge between cities and doing what works for each locality. Take social dining, the new trend of home restaurants. The biggest challenge for the government is to determine the tipping point from hobby to commercial sharing. For example, are we saying sharing food in your home once a week is okay, but if it's twice a week then you are running a restaurant? It is hard for the government to decide and it's a challenge for platforms, but it's crucial for regulation.

Sharing cities can show that there are new ways to adopt trends and embrace them. As a city, if you are not involved in these new trends then you can get left behind and that can affect both the city and the local citizens. I believe, future cities are sharing cities, so it's worth asking, 'How can we be part of that?'"

NANETTE SCHIPPERS, PROGRAMME MANAGER, SHARING ECONOMY, CITY OF AMSTERDAM, CITY HALL, AMSTERDAM.

# THE HOME COOK

**Eline Heidenrijk is 30 years old and from the Netherlands. For three years, she has cooked home-made food for people in her neighbourhood via the *Thuisafgehaald* (ShareYourMeal) platform.**

"I like to share food with people who are working till late and want to eat healthily, but don't have the time to cook for themselves. They can come and pick up food from my home. I started cooking at home when I was 12, I learnt from my mother. I always try to make everything from scratch, with fresh ingredients.

Three years ago, I started offering my home-cooked meals via the ShareYourMeal website, because friends recommended it. At first I shared portions of my surplus food. Now, it's grown and I cook regularly three to four times a week. At 8am, I list the meal online and within the hour, there will be ten people signed up, who will come later in the day to pick up the food. I have met some nice people from the neighbourhood, including older people who need regular meals and we've become friends. This platform is not only about sharing food, but about meeting your neighbours, sharing conversations with them.

When people come here for the first time, they check out my kitchen. They want to know, 'Is everything clean and tidy? Did you put something bad in my food?' You have to really trust someone to let them cook for you. I can understand it is different when you share your car, if somebody trashes your car, you won't die, you're insured. But if somebody gives you bad food, you can get food poisoning.

So food is more personal. When I have first timers here, I'm thrilled when I receive their first message saying, 'That was delicious, I'll be back for more.' Most of the cooks don't cook for the money, it's really about sharing because once you've covered the costs of ingredients, paid a commission to the platform then maybe there's a little left.

Food sharing is important to the city of Amsterdam because if you go into the subway people stare at their phones, they're very isolated from each other. It is the exact opposite when you have a Sharing platform, because suddenly people are in real contact with each other."

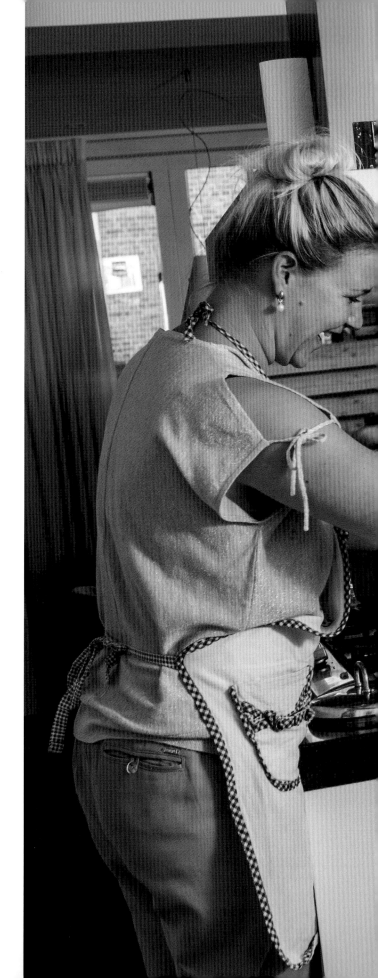

NEIGHBOUR COLLECTING FOOD FROM ELINE HEIDENRIJK, AMSTERDAM, NETHERLANDS.

"I love sharing my home-cooked food. That's why I do it, to make people happy and connected by cooking healthy meals for them and have them tell me that they love my food. We have a saying in Holland, 'Love happens through the stomach', maybe sharing happens through the stomach too?!"

# THE DINNER HOST

**"** In Italy, friendship, food and sharing are the essence of life. For me, the driver to host shared dinners is social, and if people enjoy what you are making, even better! Most people love the idea of a home restaurant, it's more intimate, more social and you make new friends. Who can resist sharing traditional Italian homemade food? **"**

**Flavia Orlando, dinner host for Share, Drink and Dine**

FLAVIA ORLANDO (60) FROM NAPLES, HOSTING A SHARED DINNER VIA
SHARING PLATFORM SHAREDnD (SHARE, DRINK AND DINE), AMSTERDAM.

# TRANSPORT SHARING

## THE BIKE SHARER

" Bike sharing is having an impact on the world's cities. You see it in Paris, London, Nice, New York – it's growing in popularity. Schemes usually use new bikes, but in Amsterdam I plan to reuse bicycles, to make better use of resources we already have. "

**Helma Shenkeveld, bike sharing campaigner**

BIKES, BOATS AND AUTOMOBILES: HELMA SCHENKEVELD (56), BIKE-SHARING CAMPAIGNER.

ERIK DE WINTER (35), FROM DUTCH ELECTRIC BIKE SHARING APP URBEE, AMSTEL.

# THE ELECTRIC BIKE SHARER

**"** There is a need for alternative, sustainable means of transportation and knowing that 80% of car rides are less than 20 km long, the electric bike is ideal for journeys between 5 and 20 km. Some of us have a utopian dream of carless cities, but first we want cities to have fewer cars. Making e-bikes available for shared use is going to be a catalyst to grow the movement of car reduction which will have a positive impact on the urban environment. **"**

**Erik de Winter, Urbee, electric bike sharing**

SHARED BIKES BY SIMON SAYS AT THE DORM, LX FACTORY, LISBON.

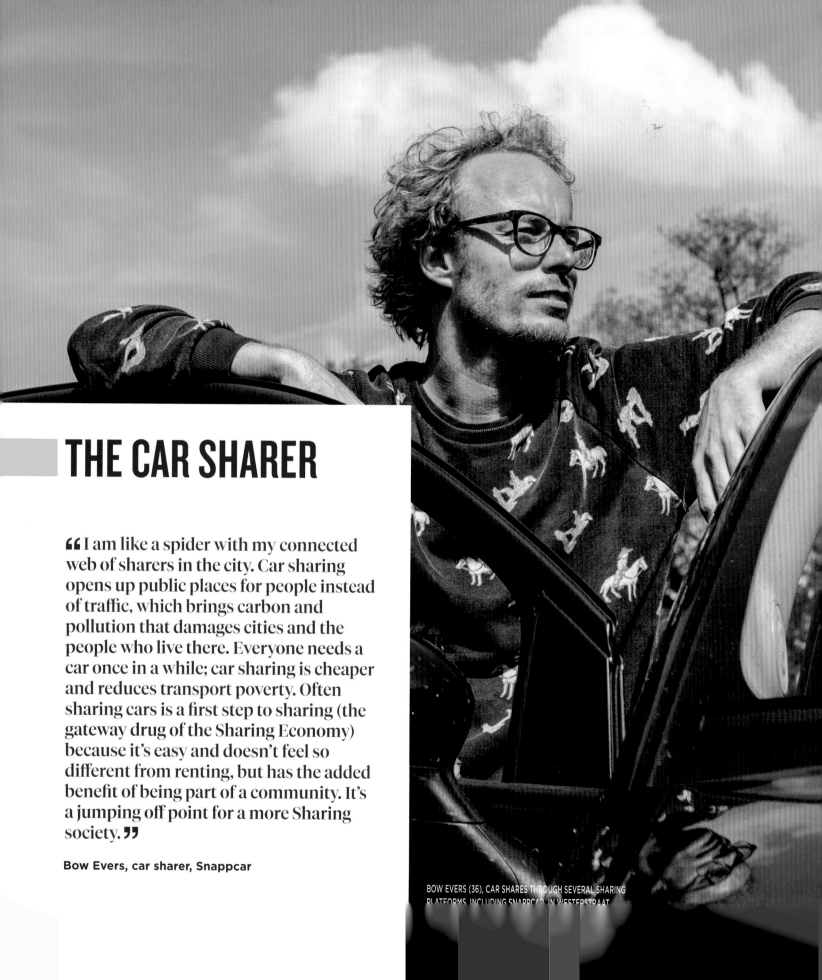

# THE CAR SHARER

"I am like a spider with my connected web of sharers in the city. Car sharing opens up public places for people instead of traffic, which brings carbon and pollution that damages cities and the people who live there. Everyone needs a car once in a while; car sharing is cheaper and reduces transport poverty. Often sharing cars is a first step to sharing (the gateway drug of the Sharing Economy) because it's easy and doesn't feel so different from renting, but has the added benefit of being part of a community. It's a jumping off point for a more Sharing society."

**Bow Evers, car sharer, Snappcar**

BOW EVERS (36), CAR SHARES THROUGH SEVERAL SHARING PLATFORMS, INCLUDING SNAPPCAR, IN WESTERSTRAAT

# THE BOAT SHARER

> **❝** In the past, possession of a boat was something only for wealthy people. Our mission is to make it accessible to everyone. Boat sharing also creates environmental impact because if we share, fewer new ones need to be manufactured. We want to introduce people to the idea that if you are an owner, you can participate in the Sharing Economy by sharing the resources that you already own. **❞**

**Floris van Hoogenhuyze, founder Barqo boat sharing**

FOUNDER OF BOAT-SHARING COMPANY BARQO, FLORIS VAN HOOGENHUYZE (29), KEIZERSGRACHT, AMSTERDAM.

# THE GOODS SHARER

**Daan Wedderpohl** is 36 years old from the Netherlands and founded the world's most successful goods Sharing platform, *Peerby*.

"We live in a world of abundance and sharing is about creating access, so we can use what's there in an efficient way. Peerby allows consumers to borrow from others nearby. I founded it in 2009 after my house burned down. In 24 hours, I lost my home, my belongings, my job (the car that came with my job) and my relationship ended. I had nothing, I was terrified. I had always been independent and thought I didn't need help. I discovered people love to help if you are willing to show your vulnerability. That changed my perspective. I had always enjoyed building software and wanted to create a company that would influence how we live. I decided to do this with consumer goods because the stuff we consume is the biggest contributor to our environmental footprint.

I want everyone in the world to share. The ultimate goal is that consumer goods will never be designed for one person, but for a community and if goods can be passed from person to person, then the manufacturers will have to create a business model where instead of manufacturing products to become obsolete, they will make things for sustainability, reparability and reuse.

Like many Sharing platforms, enabling people to go beyond consumerism and share has been challenging but we are finding ways to nudge people into new behaviour. It's frustrating that we are creating social and environmental value but this value is not counted by society. If I was able to monetise all the value we create, I would have a billion dollars.

The best way to think of a city is like the largest warehouse in the world. There are all these unused products in our homes, a bigger supply than all the commercial supply combined, everything we need is available. Owning is finite and sharing is infinite, but people in cities are isolated from each other, making it harder to share. The biggest direct result of Peerby is that people are amazed at how trustworthy and loving people actually are. I have become a very optimistic pessimist. If we deal with resource scarcity through sharing and reduce our carbon emissions, we can solve the grave challenges that we face over the next 40–50 years."

DAAN WEDDERPOHL, ROOFTOP, ROCKSTART SPACES CO-WORKING, AMSTERDAM.

REVIVE AND THRIVE: (THIS PAGE) MEN'S TOILETS WITH LIVING WALL, LXFACTORY, LISBON; (TOP RIGHT) MEMBERS OF THE MUSLALA COLLECTIVE FOR URBAN RENEWAL, ROOF TERRACE, CLAL BUILDING, JERUSALEM; (BELOW) RECYCLED PAN LIDS, LXFACTORY, LISBON; DAVID BESHUTAF (34), JERUSALEM FOOD COOPERATIVE, CLAL BUILDING, JERUSALEM, ISRAEL.

# THE REGENERATORS

❝ Our food cooperative in Jerusalem aims to take responsibility for consumer consumption. We try to add value by being more ecological, fairer and more driven by community beliefs. Our whole system is based on sharing, we manage things democratically, share the same ideology and work together. We keep costs low and are able to sell the food at a cheaper price because we buy directly from the suppliers. We remove waste from the system by being efficient and only buy what we need. We act consciously, for the benefit of the city. ❞

**David Beshutaf (34) Jerusalem Food Cooperative**

**❝** At WEconomize, we are helping organisations and municipalities design, plan and operate Sharing platforms, from shared mobility, community engagement and SMEs, to food waste, real estate, co-living and complementary currencies design. We have just launched ShareHubIL, an urban tech accelerator, focused on Sharing Economy initiatives. We will connect local sharing platforms to municipalities and help solve urban challenges such as traffic congestion and social inclusion. We view the Sharing Economy as an important strategic tool that can improve efficiency and effectively match unmet needs with underutilised assets and resources. **❞**

**Yair Freedman (41), co-founder of WEconomize, Israel**

Another City
Is Possible

"We are on a renovated rooftop that we call the 'new urbanism'. It's the home of the Muslala community. It was an abandoned space, an old shopping mall, that we turned into a place full of life. This is now one of the biggest open spaces for the public and shows how people can live together in a city, to reimagine, regenerate and rebuild it on a scale never previously imagined. We want to show that another type of city is possible, one built for the future. We all have insecurities in life, we all fear getting old and having nothing, yet we accumulate as many possessions as we can. Sharing counteracts these fears, it's saying the more we share, the more everyone will have. By sharing we create security for us all and take away the need for insecurity."

**Matan Israeli, Muslala Collective for urban renewal**

MATAN ISRAELI, MUSLALA COLLECTIVE FOR URBAN
RENEWAL, CLAL BUILDING ROOFTOP, JERUSALEM.

# THE COMMUNITY CHAMPIONS

❝ Being involved in a community composting project is transforming our urban environment. We have learned about the impact we have. Non-organic waste, like plastic, destroys our land; we don't want plastic everywhere. When I buy cheese it's put in plastic, I refuse the plastic and the shopkeeper asks why. I've told him that it takes 100 years for the earth to break it down. Knowing this makes our souls more powerful and opens our mind to things we never knew about our land and our society. Sharing is a way of healing, it's a way of changing for the better. Now people see us as leaders, sharing and leading change. ❞

**Maha Sbeih, community leader, Sur Baher Community Centre**

PALESTINIAN WOMEN, SUR BAHER COMMUNITY CENTRE,
EAST JERUSALEM. (L TO R), MEIRVT NIMER, SUHEIR ABU TER,
KIVELLY ATTON, MAHA SBEIH, WAFA MAHMOUD ATTON.

# THE FUTURE OF WORK

**"** The trend will be fewer traditional offices with less power and scale. Co-working, shared working, will become much more important and mainstream. That's because people want to be a part of a community, part of a crowd. **"**

**Sergi Tarragona, founder, Cloud Co-Working, Barcelona**

Flexible, adaptable, collaborative: these are the skills that we need for the future. The amount of data we are sharing is overwhelming; every minute we send 29 million WhatsApp messages, carry out 240,000 Google searches, and share 3.2 billion images every day.[67] 65% of children entering primary school today will work in jobs that haven't yet been invented and it's debatable whether, in the future, the concept of a job will exist at all.

Even if it does, most of us will have been replaced by robots, with the outlook being particularly grim for accountants who have a 97% chance of losing their jobs to golem.[68] The notion of a 9 to 5 office-based job-for-life has been replaced by gig working, remote working and co-working, a now global movement of workspace Sharing.

THE FUTURE OF WORK: RECYCLED SIGNAGE, LX FACTORY, LISBON.

VILLAGE UNDERGROUND CO-WORKING, LX FACTORY, LISBON; FABCAFE
CO-WORKING, BARCELONA; BOOK SHARING AT KUBIK, BARCELONA.

" Kubik began like most interesting stories. It was late, it was night, we were drunk. A friend had rented a space on the third floor of this building, we decided to start working here, but on different projects. Then our friend moved. Suddenly, we were like, 'What do we do with 300 square metres?' So we invited friends from other countries to share the space. "

**Miquel Lacasta**

# THE CO-WORKING CREATORS

**Miquel Lacasta (52) and Javi Creus (54) from Spain, created *Kubik*, the world's first co-working space in Barcelona, in 1994.**

**Javi:** We dreamt someday we would have the whole building and it would host people with different skills. We came up with the name KUBIK which is an acronym for Kultural Universal Basic Ideas and Koncepts.

**Miquel:** If you give energy to a space, it will give you back the energy to do something new. It's sharing.

**Javi:** We were doing something different; we were competing against isolation, creating a nurturing environment that offers better conversations than working from home and a community. The community started to grow, as did the media interest. We were branded 'hippies'. On the middle floor, there was a factory that went bankrupt and we took on the second floor. The ground floor was a chocolate factory; that also closed and we took that over, giving us the whole building. We didn't have rules, policies or contracts, but we developed five principles. Life is a premise. Innovation is our strategy. Technology is an opportunity. Complexity is a weapon of challenge. Collaboration and cooperation are dynamic things.

**Miquel:** Our ethos is that we need to experiment to see how change happens and what role we play in the change to benefit ourselves, our community and our cities.

**Javi:** We created an ecosystem and when the species becomes too big it has to leave to grow. Sometimes, success means leaving.

**Miquel:** When we first came here, there was no life in this neighbourhood. Now, the area is bustling with life. We have 100 people coming in to work every day and 50 coming in for meetings.

**Javi:** If we found the right partner, we would replicate this, we would have Kubiks everywhere, but we would want to replicate the culture. Sometimes we say that we are the world trade centre of the little companies. **"**

KUBIK CO-WORKING FOUNDERS, (L TO R) MIQUEL LACASTA AND JAVI CREUS, BARCELONA.

# THE CO-WORKING INNOVATOR

"The design of the space is key to increasing the sharing potential between members, the first impression is like a WOW effect. We have a lot of natural light, because that is important for the co-worker, it is where you spend most of your time. People tell me that this space gives them a reason to come to work every morning. It is about being in an environment with a community that makes you want to come back tomorrow. Co-working definitely increases productivity, people get more done because they collaborate. They're inspired to be more creative, they feel less stressed, more relaxed."

**Sergei Tarragona, founder, Cloud Co-working**

SERGEI TARRAGONA (26), FOUNDER OF CLOUD CO-WORKING, ONE OF THE LARGEST CO-WORKING SPACES IN SPAIN; (R) CO-WORKERS, LOUNGE SPACE, CLOUD CO-WORKING, BARCELONA.

**Africa Middle Classes**

A photographic journey through the middle classes.

This work won a World Press Photo published in 28 countries.

Jean Bardeletti is a French engineer and professional based.

MARKOS PAPATHEODOROU (3), PLAYING
ON MOUNT PYXARIA, HOME OF THE
STAGONES COLLECTIVE, EVIA, GREECE.

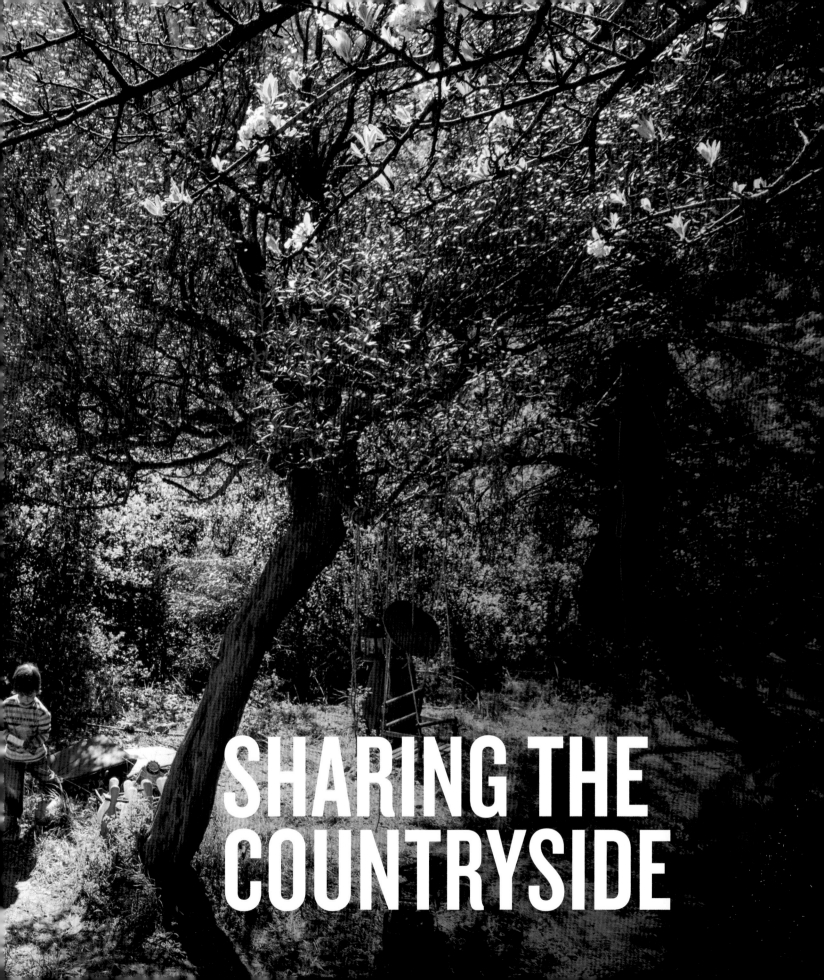

# SHARING THE COUNTRYSIDE

f the notion of idyllic, peaceful country life appeals, just imagine combining all that greenery with a Sharing lifestyle. That's what Giorgos Vallis did when he left the 'madding' crowds of Athens and headed for his birthplace Paliomylos, on the Greek island of Evia. His mission: to build a rural eco-farm and self-sustaining community based on the principles of Sharing and permaculture. Giorgos is not alone in his vision (well of course not, he's sharing). In fact, escaping the city is a dream many urbanites have. By 2025, it's predicted that in the UK alone, half a million of them will have abandoned urban life to move to the countryside.[69] And it's easy to understand why. Rural lifestyles are reportedly healthier, wealthier and happier,[70] with 31% of people saying they 'love' the area in which they live, compared to just 16% in cities.[71] But is there something more significant at the heart of this rural migration and the lure of pastures new?

Gandhi described the village as 'the soul of India', a place of authenticity, community and cooperation. In India, the village is a place where Sharing is such an innate aspect of life, there isn't even a local word for it. Country living is often characterised by strong social bonds, as Hillary Bee from Time to Breathe, Totnes, says, 'It is easier to share in a smaller place where the networking is much deeper. You share with someone in multi-layered ways. You don't just see them in one context. You have seen their cousin, you have gone dancing with their brother and you know who they dated. There is a depth of information which makes sharing easier.'

Indeed, many Sharing traditions can be traced back to the countryside. Hitchhiking is an original form of ride-sharing and 'gleaning' is a custom originating in the Old Testament, where leftover crops were collected from farmers' fields following a harvest. The New Deal era in 1930s America saw the birth of electricity and phone cooperatives among farming communities, making the amenities affordable through sharing. Indeed, this reliance on others and a culture of Sharing is inherent to village life where, traditionally, each person contributes something – a skill, job or resource – to make up a micro-sharing economy. While this might seem like a romanticised view of rustic existence, it is precisely these reasons cited when inhabitants are asked why they choose to live there and why those escaping the city want to take up rural residency.

Despite an initial urban focus, tech-enabled Sharing is expanding to rural areas, with 15% of Sharing platforms focusing their activities outside cities.[72] Technology that takes the pain out of farming, known as AgTech, is on the rise, with Sharing marketplaces proving popular; from Australia's farmer-to-farmer equipment rental sites, Agtribe and FarmBit, to on-demand FarmBackup in Denmark. Nigeria and Kenya are home to Hello Tractor, which have created a new generation of rural micro-entrepreneurs, while Ghana's TroTro Tractor can track machinery in real-time. In India, AgroStar and TRRINGO are marketplaces for accessing shared farming equipment.

Villages are, in many ways, models for the Sharing Economy. Indeed, the technology-driven 'global village' that author Marshall McLuhan predicted in the 1960s has come to fruition today.[73] One view is that the Sharing Economy itself is a glorified, online village but, as the *Generation Share* stories show, the phenomenon is not restricted to online Sharing, it pervades every aspect of life. What's true is that digital Sharing activity mimics rural life, taking its inspiration from the source.

# THE CITY ESCAPEE

**Giorgos Vallis is 36 and from the island of Evia in Greece. He is building an eco-community and organic farm called *Paliomylos*.**

"I was exasperated with city life and of having a job as an employee. I was just giving more money to rich people and feeling unfulfilled. Then I came back to Evia, to Paliomylos. This house was a watermill 200 years ago and I decided to rebuild it and create a community.

We made an effort to design the garden based on permaculture principles. Permaculture is a way that you can make agriculture not only sustainable, but it improves and contributes to the land. It's a type of sharing. It's not just sharing between humans, it's sharing the planet, with everything around us, animals and plants. Usually, we just concentrate on the social and our human surroundings, but the important thing is to find balance to be able to live on this planet for the long term. This happens in permaculture, because your waste is the food of something else that you never thought about, so everything we don't eat, the chickens eat, then the chickens give us back eggs, so we share our existence. If you don't share, then you shouldn't expect to get back.

Modern society in a city makes you alone. Even though you see millions of people around you, you don't connect with anybody because everybody has their own room, their own things, their own phone and laptop and want more things to fill up this life, which feels like a 'void'. If you change that and start socialising with other people, sharing the same things you realise that it's better to be surrounded by people you share with and to own less.

Sharing is re-evaluating your needs and your perception of yourself, realising that you aren't more important than others, that everybody should get a part of everything and you shouldn't necessarily have more. Sharing is understanding that wanting to have more, takes you further away from others. If you want to be close then you have to share even though you have materially fewer things, you have a more fulfilled life."

BREAKFAST AT PALIOMYLOS WITH MOMO, HARRIS, GIORGOS, EMMA AND JEAN-CHRISTOPH, EVIA, GREECE; EMMA AND HARRIS MAKING PIZZA; GIORGOS VALLIS IN HIS ECO TOOL SHED; STONE OUTHOUSE FOR BIKE AND TOOL STORAGE, PALIOMYLOS, EVIA, GREECE.

# THE VILLAGE SHARER

**Inir Pinheiro** is 37 years old and from Mumbai in India. He is the founder of *Grassroutes*, a social enterprise that improves villagers' livelihoods through community-based tourism services. Established in 2006, *Grassroutes* has worked with over 3,000 villagers.

" We work with villagers to design tours and shared experiences that benefit both villagers and those who visit them. Previously, the only time a rural person would meet a city person was when they travelled to the city and found the dirty, congested, urban environments alienating and not conducive to building relationships. These programmes have given the villagers a sustainable income; now they see a 35% increase in annual earnings. For women, this means independence, they can work, support elderly parents and the girls are able to tell their parents that they do not want to be married at 16.

The tours help city people learn and experience the joy of simplicity. A Japanese visitor was shocked that the villagers did not have watches. She asked them how they knew the time. They told her that when they felt hungry they ate and when they were tired they slept. The visitor said she was constantly working to a schedule and this was an entirely different world for her.

In village communities, sharing is an intrinsic part of life. It's like breathing, it isn't conscious. Even the land they live on belongs to everyone; there's no individual ownership. In some communities, people barely have half a piece of bread to eat, but they will offer you half of it. They don't see scarcity, they see abundance. When you sit down and interact with village people, you learn a lot about sharing. Last year, a woman's husband and child were in an accident. The entire village came together to take them to hospital and pay for the medical expenses. In the city, you're lucky if the family come to visit you in hospital.

IT TAKES A VILLAGE: INIR PINHEIRO WITH VILLAGERS, GRASSROUTES PROJECT, DEHNA, INDIA.

MEGHNA RAJPOPAT (38), VISITOR BEING
WELCOMED TO DEHNA VILLAGE, INDIA.

CHANDRABHAGA PATELLAR AT HOME, DEHNA VILLAGE, MAHARASHTRA, INDIA.

We've seen the impact of these programmes and the sharing goes both ways. One of the village women said, 'I am pleased that the tourists come to our village, because in the safety of my home, my grandchildren can interact with people from the rest of the world. We are getting a glimpse of how the entire world lives.'

The biggest transformation we have seen is in the city people. India is very rural, but politically it is very dominated by urban culture and the urban mindset plays a huge role in government policies. People in cities are often indifferent to what happens in villages. By virtue of creating a Sharing platform, the people of urban India can finally put a face to a farmer. 🞂🞂

"The urban culture of sharing stems from separateness; in a rural culture, it stems from togetherness. People in cities share something to appear generous. In villages there's an awareness that we are all same, we are all human, we all need to eat, be joyful, get our work done. Sharing is what you do. In the city, sharing has become transactional, whereas in villages, people don't know how to react when you give them money for an act of kindness. They say, 'Why can't you just enjoy what you've been given? There is no need to pay me. When it's your turn, do something good and pass it on to someone else.' 🞂🞂

**Megna Rajpopat, Grassroutes participant**

# THE NATURAL SHARER

**Natalia Iliadi** is 32 years old and from Greece. She is part of *Stagones*, a rural collective of eco-architects, who live and work on Mount Pyxaria on the island of Evia. The group participate in what they call an 'exchange economy', working with nature, recycling materials, skill swapping and empowering the local community through the structures they help to build.

"Sharing is an everyday thing here, we share our lives. The idea was to enjoy a simpler life, to live and work in nature. Evia is a quite an undeveloped area of Greece, and seemed like an ideal playground for our unconventional building and living experiments.

We build using natural materials as a collective. We work together in a very organic way. It's not about making balls of mud and straw with other people; it's about working together towards a common goal, sharing a journey with joint aspirations. This is what creates strong bonds between us. It's an agile process and it's hard to distinguish the design stage from the building stage, we experiment as we create. Natural materials are malleable, so if you make a mistake, you can redo it, unlike concrete.

You don't need to sit by yourself in an office and spend hours trying to solve problems that you have not yet encountered. Trying to project the needs of a person is what people do in an architect's office. We bring the team and the client on location, to develop the design together in a hands-on way, it's truly collaborative. Recently, we had a violinist from Switzerland who wanted a remote studio house, a place she could come to compose her music. She collaborated with us on the design and she loves the end result.

As a team, we share time and space; we live on two pieces of land that are close to each other. We work together, sometimes dine together and play music in the evenings. Every now and again, we build something collectively for ourselves or for the village community. It's a special place where you can feel the magic of sharing."

FORCE OF NATURE: NATALIA ILIADI; OUTDOOR DINING, STAGONES DESIGN, MOUNT PYXARIA, EVIA.
OVERLEAF: (L TO R) MARKOS PAPATHEODOROU, NATALIA ILIADI, ZOE PAPACHRISTOU, YIANNIS PAPATHEODOROU AND NIKOS KOTONIKAS, AT HOME, MOUNT PYXARIA, EVIA, GREECE; MARKOS PAPATHEODOROU; LIVING ROOF BY STAGONES COLLECTIVE; WITHOUT WALLS: ECO BATHROOM.

# TRANSITION TOWNS

**❝** Transition means a shift away from dependency on oil, which is a finite resource, towards a sustainable, caring, sharing society, where everyone's needs are met within the planet's limits. **❞**

**Larch Maxey, Network of Wellbeing, Totnes**

**❝** Sharing our stuff, buying less stuff and sharing cars all help to reduce our carbon dioxide emissions, playing a part in helping to solve climate change problems. **❞**

**Mark Jefferys, Share Shed, Transition Town Totnes**

The transition town movement began its life in 2005 and emerged from the work of permaculture educator Rob Hopkins and his students Louise Rooney and Catherine Dunne. 2006 saw Hopkins return to his home town of Totnes in Devon to establish the world's first transition town. A transition town is a colourful collage of local, community-led, crowd-sourced initiatives, designed to reimagine and rebuild the world sustainably and address the big global challenges we face. Sharing is at the heart of the transition philosophy where you'll find low impact affordable housing, skills sharing, CSAs (community supported agriculture), swap shops, local currencies, book crossings and food grown locally in unusual places. Characterised by bottom-up community-led action, the movement is about reclaiming the economy and creating webs of connection and support. It has now spread to over 50 countries, with thousands of transition initiatives in towns, villages, cities, universities and schools worldwide.[74]

LOOK TO THE FUTURE: TRANSITION TOWN, TOTNES, UK.

# THE SHED SHARER

**Mark Jefferys** is 56 and from the UK. He runs the Totnes *Share Shed* in Devon, UK, a 'library of things' where people can borrow tools and other equipment they need. The *Share Shed* is a project of the *Network of Wellbeing*.

" The Share Shed is trying to cut down on stuff that people buy by sharing and borrowing instead. I want people to think, 'Could I borrow that instead of buying it?' The Shed is about encouraging sharing so we become a more resourceful and connected community.

I was out in nature all the time as a child. I did an ecology degree; my work is about connecting kids with the natural world and I cannot envisage living any other way. The transition movement and the Share Shed is a practical application of living in harmony with the planet. A big part of the transition way of living is about cutting down on oil dependency, borrowing rather than buying helps reduce our impact on the planet.

Cities have a lot more people and stuff to share. But the actual connection of people may be difficult in cities where people do not know their neighbours. In rural areas, traditionally, people share and know each other. In Totnes, we are getting back to that and the Share Shed helps. I feel we are at a turning point and a number of people who use the Shed have realised that they don't need to buy stuff anymore. So far the most popular item is the strimmer and the most unusual thing people can borrow is the unicycle, although the lawn aerators that you strap on to your boots come a close second! If there were Share Sheds everywhere, it would transform our world. It's an idea whose time has come. "

MARK JEFFERYS, SHARE SHED, TOTNES, UK.

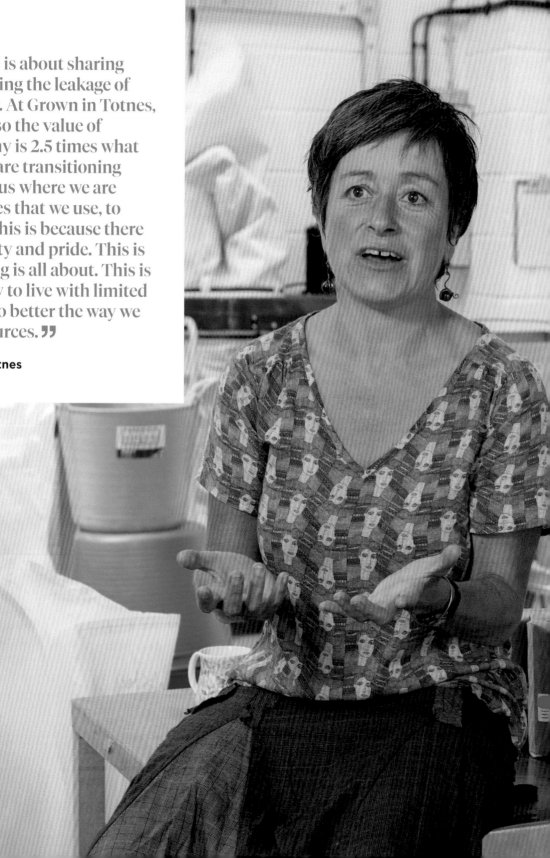

# THE HARVEST SHARER

"Transition Town Totnes is about sharing resources, skills and reducing the leakage of money out of the economy. At Grown in Totnes, we support local growers, so the value of money to the local economy is 2.5 times what it would be otherwise. We are transitioning away from the current status where we are removed from the resources that we use, to being intricately related. This is because there is traceability, responsibility and pride. This is what transition and sharing is all about. This is the way to understand how to live with limited resources. If we are going to better the way we live, we need to share resources."

**Holly Tiffen, founder, Grown in Totnes**

TRANSITION TOWN TOTNES: HOLLY TIFFEN (45)
FOUNDER OF GROWN IN TOTNES; GROWN IN
TOTNES; TOTNES POUND, SEEDS 2 BAKERY.

# THE EDIBLE SHARERS

❝I believe in Incredible Edible, a project that grows free food in public spaces for everyone to share. Locals appreciate having a place where they are free to take whatever they want. I remember once, we planted almond trees, a woman picked a bag full of almonds from the ground. She was not able to believe her luck and said that she was going to keep them till Christmas and share with friends and neighbours. That real engagement with the life around us is the reason I do this.❞

**Wendy Stayte, Incredible Edible**

❝The first time I noticed this place I found edible salads. Totnes is a town that has so much that is open to people. The whole idea of growing food that anybody could get access to illustrates who we are as people. We want you to come here and be happy. We grow all these beautiful vegetables and you can come here and help yourselves. There is nothing expected of you. You don't have to volunteer. It is all about sharing.❞

**Syvila Chaplin, Incredible Edible**

INCREDIBLE EDIBLE PLANTER, TOTNES RAILWAY STATION; INCREDIBLE EDIBLE, RAISED BEDS, STEAMER QUAY; INCREDIBLE EDIBLE TOTNES VOLUNTEERS, (L TO R) MELANIE COTTERILL (51), SYVILA CHAPLIN (60), JOHN JEFFREYS (37), WENDY STAYTE (76), STEAMER QUAY.

# THE INNER SHARER

❝Inner sharing is understanding, it's sharing space together; it is even when we don't necessarily agree with someone, but we can be in the same space with them in an open way. Inner transition is very important. It's about creating a new social model. If we do not reflect, we are just going to replicate structures with dreadful dynamics where individuals have power over each other. This would not happen if we do some inner work. If we practice inner sharing.❞

**Hillary Bee, Time to Breathe, Totnes**

TIME TO BREATHE, A GROUP FOR INNER TRANSITION, VIRE ISLAND, TOTNES, UK

SHARING
THE MONEY

Imagine a world built on food justice, empowerment and equality. A world where success means belonging to a community, making a meaningful contribution to society and enjoying abundance in return; where business is a force for good and operates within the limits of the planet, where we repair what we have and where we are all philanthropists of the heart. In this world, community is king and money is meaningless. We've stopped measuring the production of goods and started measuring happiness and wellbeing. We've stopped obsessing over quantity, contracts and outputs, and we've begun to focus on the value created for people and planet. This is a universe where life is about thriving, and true prosperity brings social and environmental growth; where all value – economic, social and environmental – is costed and counted, where one doesn't ride roughshod over the other and where our actions have 'zero marginal cost'[75] to all who live here.

The people who feature in *Generation Share* are already living in this world, they cherish a different kind of wealth. It's a reality beyond carbon, it may be built on blockchain,[76] where local currencies bring value to those who contribute and citizen innovation is commonplace. They know how important equality is, that unless we reach our optimum 'spirit level' we all suffer – especially the wealthy. Many enjoy the benefits of 'plugging and playing into the Internet of Things';[77] they trade directly, person-to-person, cutting out the corporate middlemen, creating new business models that bring tripartite value for all genders, races, religions and people. In their world, the favourite pastime is Sharing, not shopping.

This new wealth creation isn't just for those who are already wealthy. The Sharing Economy has been shown to create three times the social impact for low-income communities.[78] Sharing services that offer access to affordable meals, healthcare and medical equipment are disproportionately benefiting low-income groups who often spend higher proportions of pay on these basics.[79] Car Sharing alleviates transport poverty[80] and food Sharing programmes offer meals to the hungry.[81]

So, can we flourish within the limits of our planet? Can we create a post-capitalist system, a true Sharing Economy where all value matters and where true wealth means inclusion, love and respect? Can we, as Paul Hawken asks, 'create a remarkably different economy, one that can restore eco-systems and protect the environment while bringing forth innovation, prosperity, meaningful work and true security?' Can ecology and commerce make peace with one another? And what about our consumer addiction, can we kick it? The answer? Yes, we can. We can escape our 'iron cage of consumerism' to a world where we can 'come and spread (our) arms if (we) really need a hug'.[82]

'Can we kick it?' Oh yes, we can, and *Generation Share* already has.

# THE CHANGE-MAKER

**Aarti Naik** is 29 years old and from the Mulund slum in Mumbai, India. She set up *Sakhi School for Girls Education* to empower slum-based girls and their mothers.

" I grew up living in a slum community with no education or support for girls. The schools in India teach in Hindi or English and in the slum we speak the Marathi dialect, so we aren't able to understand what we are being taught. Like many girls around me, I became a school dropout. I didn't know how to read, write or do maths and my parents were unable to pay fees for private tuition. I had no choice but to work. I was making necklaces, earning 9 rupees (10p) a day. I knew that education was my escape, so I saved up and used the money to help me pass my exams.

The slums are a difficult environment to grow up in because parents have to focus on survival rather than education. Girls end up working and marrying at a young age, or being sold into prostitution. That's why I wanted to start the Sakhi School for Girls. The word 'sakhi' means 'a female friend who inspires, guides, and supports other girls for a good cause'. My mum had struggled all her life but she passed on her determined spirit and inspired me. First, I had to teach myself to be a teacher. My mum helped me start the Sakhi School from our tiny two-room slum home because I had no access to a space or finance. The whole idea is based on sharing. I shared our space with five girls from the slum, sharing my own experience by teaching them what I knew.

GIRL POWER: AARTI NAIK WITH HER MOTHER PUSHPA IN THEIR ONE-ROOM HOME, MULUND, MUMBAI, INDIA.

EAT, PRAY, LEARN: SAKHI SCHOOL FOR GIRLS: VAISHALI, STUDENT MOTHER.

I heard about the Ashoka organisation for change-makers, who help to finance projects. I contacted them, shared my vision and they were inspired by my story. They gave me a year of support to open a school and I was able to rent a small room to teach girls in. I decided to teach the basics: Hindi, English and maths. We also teach financial literacy and help the girls save money for their education, one rupee at a time. To encourage girls to come here, we share a hot meal with them every day, so they know if they come to the Sakhi School they won't go hungry.

I've had to learn about management and how to network and connect with people outside the slum area. I won an Ashoka change-maker award, it really boosted my confidence. Then I discovered UnLtd India, an organisation that supports social entrepreneurs and they also helped me to achieve my vision. Now I teach 300 slum-based girls and their mothers.

Sharing is very important to the girls. I share my life experiences with them and their mothers, to build confidence. Previously they had no place where they could talk and share emotions, happiness, dreams or problems. We've created a space and opportunity to talk. Since I started the Sakhi School in 2008, no girl here has dropped out. Every girl goes to school confidently and passes her exams every year. It's created a big impact, you support, share your experience and your life and you change others. I decided to teach mothers too because I realised that they didn't know how to read or how to teach their children. Now they can read and write.

My work will always be with the slum community. I will stay in Mulund, I love the hospitality, this is my birthplace. My vision is for every girl to go to school confidently and to have a Sakhi School for Girls in every slum area in India. In the next 5 years, I'd like to educate 1,000 girls. "

(L TO R), JIA, PRIYANKA, RIYA AND YSHVI PRAYING.

**❝** Coming to Sakhi has made me much more confident, more independent. I enjoy coming here and love to learn new things. **❞**

**Komal (19), a student at Sakhi School for Girls Education**

FOOD FROM THE COMMUNITY SERVED BY PRAMILA.

AARTI NAIK TEACHING PRERANA.

**❝** Sharing is very important, you get help, emotional support and a learning experience. It's a safe space. My girls are happy with the education, they get to play and eat here. For me, now that I have learned Hindi and English at Sakhi, I can communicate with the doctor. If I have a health problem, I can understand what they are telling me. **❞**

**Shaila Gi Kaleti (41), participant, Mothers' Programme, Sakhi School for Girls Education**

**❝** I was inspired by Aarti's story, so I decided to help. I love it here. Sharing is about increasing other people's knowledge and distributing it. **❞**

**Sindhu Ramdas Kendre (31), maths and English teacher-trainer, Sakhi School for Girls Education**

# THE CITIZEN INNOVATOR

**Georgia Haddad Nicolau** is 31 years old and from Sao Paolo, Brazil. She is the Director of the *Procomum Institute* in Sao Paolo and a leader in the citizen innovation movement. Citizen innovation is where the citizens themselves co-create solutions that impact their lives.

"True innovation does not exist without sharing. If you do not open up and share, it is not innovative because innovation is something that changes, it is a living thing. Citizen innovation is about creating a network between individuals, ideas and infrastructure. Innovation is not about institutions, it is about creativity in scarcity, in poverty, based on people's needs. If people have the right infrastructure, ideas and individuals, then they can do citizen innovation. It happens at a grass-roots level.

We embrace failure, we see life as a process, you do not need to have things perfectly ready to go. Everything we do is open-licensed, people can share information. We document the process using technology so that the learning continues. It is not only creating solutions, but creating bonds and empathy, remembering that we are all humans and have the means to think for ourselves.

The impact of citizen innovation is seen through entrepreneurship; it's about people developing their own solutions. We focus on how to experiment with new and alternative ways of what inclusion and poverty means. If we continue to exclude people, there is no systemic change. We research alternative ways of living and ask questions like, 'How much money do we need to live? Can we use time banks, social currencies, Sharing Economy platforms and ideas?' If people are focused on consumption rather than citizenship, poverty will continue to be a problem. You see this happen, when the economy is good, people consume more, but you go to the favelas and they have a television but no electricity, no sanitation, no education."

GEORGIA HADDAD NICOLAU, CO-DIRECTOR OF PROCOMUM INSTITUTE, SAO PAOLO.

" We work on the concept of a commons-based economy. We have experiments where people are creating their own money, building their own neighbourhoods, growing their own food in community gardens. There's a whole ecosystem that is developing and growing based on citizen innovation. It's ground up, created by citizens to build the future they want and need. "

# THE FOOD JUSTICE CAMPAIGNER

Malik Yakitini is 61 years old, from the USA and the founder of the *Detroit Black Food Security Network*, which runs a 7-acre community site called *D-Town Farm*.

" Sharing means seeing another human being as an extension of yourself. We are bought into individuality, we say, 'I am different and separate from you'. In reality, we are like one organism, and sharing is like seeing a larger, collective self as its essence.

There are four aspects to food justice. The first is having access to high-quality food regardless of economic status. The second is that people working in the food system should be fairly treated. Currently, those who harvest food are paid wages that are deplorable and work in horrible conditions. Thirdly, community members should see the economic benefits of the money that someone pays for food. In my community, people from outside run the stores and money is stripped out of the community. Fourthly, we are not separate from the animals and the birds who we share this earth with. Part of food justice is growing food that is sustainable so that we are good citizens of this earth.

There are many challenges for the African American community in accessing food. There is very poor public transportation in Detroit and 40% of people do not have cars. So the food that you have access to is the food that is in walking distance – often highly processed junk food. And, if good food is available, but you cannot afford to buy it, you don't have access to it. Food justice has to be coupled with the struggle against poverty, food is a human right. As a human being, regardless of your economic status, race, gender or religion, you have the right to high-quality food, just as you have a right to water.

We live in a capitalist system where everything is commoditised and access depends on wealth. There is a rampant individualistic mindset prevalent in capitalism and this greed (the not-sharing) is the root of poverty. I am working hard to dismantle it and to create another system that is more equitable. The way out of it is to see each other as an extension of ourselves so, sharing is natural like in your family.

Often it is the preparation and consumption of food which is done communally. That is how human bonds are built. So the sharing of food is fundamental to reknitting the social fabric. Campaigning for food justice is why I was put on this earth. I am blessed with the kind of work I do every day. I have discovered my purpose in life. "

MALIK YAKITINI, FOUNDER OF THE DETROIT BLACK FOOD SECURITY NETWORK DETROIT, USA.

Ιατρείο
Κοινωνικής
Αλληλεγγύης
Περιστερίου

# A PEOPLE'S WEALTH SYSTEM

Faced with austerity and economic exclusion due to debt and rising unemployment (the highest in Europe), communities in Greece have been building what they call a 'solidarity economy'. A response to the socioeconomic-turned-humanitarian crisis, this cooperative, autonomous, self-organised and self-managed solidarity movement has built an alternative system providing housing, food and healthcare to those who need them most. By taking matters into their own hands, these people-powered projects are saving lives every day.

Following a 2012 law prohibiting access to public healthcare for uninsured Greeks, over 60 solidarity clinics that serve over 80,000 people have sprung up in Athens alone.[83] The clinics operate without money, with doctors, nurses and support workers sharing their time. Abandoned buildings have become doctor's surgeries, surplus medicines that would otherwise end up in landfill are put to good use, and idle medical equipment is given a second life so it too can save lives.

What began as an emergency response to the collapse of Greece's capitalist, commoditised, inhumane economy is becoming a socioeconomic system in its own right, one that is led by and for the people.

SOLIDARITY CLINIC, PERISTERI, ATHENS, GREECE.

# THE SHARING DOCTOR

**Dr Olga Kesidou** is a 52-year-old ear, nose and throat specialist from Greece. Along with 15 other medics, including a paediatrician, orthopaedic surgeon and a cardiologist, she volunteers at the *Solidarity Clinic of Peristeri*, treating patients who cannot afford to see a doctor.

"A person shares from the moment they are born. You share your toys, your room, your food. Life is all about sharing. If you don't share, life has no purpose. If you are alone in heaven, you are alone.

The clinic was set up five years ago, when people did not have access to public healthcare. They lost their jobs, their medicines and could not get insurance. So we set up a solidarity clinic. We covered the whole spectrum of medical specialties, cooperated with some doctors in the Greek NHS, because we needed specialty equipment and set up a charter with rules for how they would operate. We wanted to ensure that these clinics were for people not profit and were open and inclusive to all races, genders and religions. We set up a food drive and a social kitchen where we would cook at home, and bring food to share because we realised that people didn't just need medicines, they needed to eat.

We had a girl who came in, she was uninsured, unemployed, she was embarrassed and ashamed of her situation. She was treated, she got better. Afterwards, she offered to help us, she wanted to give back. We are a community, we share feelings, we share the satisfaction that we are doing our duty. We are professionals and we receive a lot of love from society and we want to remind them that they are not alone. We have already achieved miracles. Our ask, that the state create legislation for the uninsured, has now become a reality, even though, five years ago, no one thought this was possible, but we fought for it. Since 2016, uninsured people can go to hospitals but we realise that refugees and others still need us. So, we are continuing.

The solidarity movement is not about charity. It is about the belief that, tomorrow, you could be in the same position as the person you are treating today. My dream is for a better society. I don't want to be paid by my patients. I want to live in dignity and share my skills to help others in need."

DR OLGA KESIDOU WITH DONATED SURPLUS MEDICINES, SOLIDARITY CLINIC, PERISTERI, ATHENS, GREECE.

# THE TRUST SHARER

"The Trust Café shows money is not the only value, there are other things more important in life, that we should be grateful for. This is a place of love, where you get more than a meal. Trust creates value and is the basis of sharing. True sharing is about giving and not expecting anything in return, it's about being open and able to trust. People come here and appreciate what goes into creating a café, from the volunteers in the kitchen, to the person who smiles at you when you walk in the door. This pay-as-you-feel place makes a positive impact on society."

**Dejan Tomaševiē (45) from Serbia, volunteer, Trust Cafe, Amsterdam, pay-as-you-feel eatery**

GRATITUDE WALL, TRUST CAFE, AMSTERDAM.

# THE REPAIR SHOP

**""** People come to Millor Que Nou! to repair things that need fixing. They can get anything that's broken mended. This space is free for local people, they can access tools, find someone who can repair their goods or learn to repair things themselves. Through repair, we give items a second life, rather than throwing them away. When people repair things, it shows respect, they feel proud of themselves, they say 'I saved it'. If people repaired more things, there would be less waste, it would be good for the environment and people living in poverty could save money. **""**

**Ana Gimēnez Lōpez, worker at Millor Que Nou!**

MILLOR QUE NOU!, COMMUNITY REPAIR SHOP, BARCELONA.

# THE VALUE SHARERS

" The Sharing Economy is a revival of old values, a return to understanding what true, human, social value is. "

**Francisco Neves, founder, Sharing platform Simon Says**

(L TO R) SIMON (37), PEDRO (40) AND FRANCISCO (32), FOUNDERS OF SIMON SAYS, A PROJECT THAT HELPS VISITORS TO VALUE THE LOCAL CULTURE, LX FACTORY, LISBON.

(RIGHT) UNIVERSITY OF BARCELONA, A MEMBER OF THE SHARING ACADEMY, THE WORLD'S FIRST MARKETPLACE FOR PEER-TO-PEER LEARNING.

# THE SHARING ACADEMY

**"** Sharing means a different type of economy that is not just based on money, where you make a human investment, rather than a financial one. That's what we do at the Sharing Academy. If you get good grades, you can help other students to pass their exams. There's all this value that's created and knowledge that can be shared. If I am studying Business Administration and am struggling in maths, I can get help from peers who have been through the same programme. So far, 1,000 students have found tutors through our platform and have passed their exams. **"**

**Albert Andreu (37), co-founder, the Sharing Academy,
the world's first marketplace for peer-to-peer learning**

# THE PHILANTHROPIST

**Payal Kothari** is 44 years old and is from Mumbai. She is a nutrition coach and philanthropist.

"My parents have always been sharers. They lived with 20 people in one room, whatever they had they would share, in an equal way, with my three sisters and the community. We were raised that sharing is about karma and reincarnation, if you share now, you'll have a good future.

I started sharing money when I was five. There was a man who would play the flute outside our apartment every Sunday. I would wrap coins in newspaper and throw them to him from the sixth floor. I never knew him, but he would look at me and play one of my favourite songs, every Sunday for 20 years.

At 16, I started teaching drama; I was paid 700 rupees a month. My philanthropy started with my first pay cheque. I shared the entire thing and divided the money between my mum, dad, sisters and my helper to buy books for her son. Seeing how much she appreciated the money gave me such happiness in return. She said, 'Nobody has ever done this for me before, we are not even blood-related'.

My driver told me that his daughters didn't have a toilet in their village home. His wife would take the children to use the toilet on the highway. I asked him if that was dangerous and he said that's what everyone does. I gave him money to build a toilet at home. As news of the toilet building spread around the village, it created a domino effect and other families started to build toilets. My driver has helped to transform his village. For me, knowing that, makes me happy.

Wealth makes me feel powerful because it means I can share. Sharing and wealth has an infinite relationship. The more money I have, the more I can share. It's very important for me to be independent, to have my own wealth, my own bank account and not be answerable to anybody. It's about having my own power to distribute my money and to give to whoever I want. If I see ten kids on the street, I want to know I can pay for a roof over their heads, food and education, then they'll be empowered and free to live the life they want.

Philanthropy means giving without expecting anything in return. I don't do this with expectations. I don't want praise, but I love feedback. I like to know the difference my money has made. It propels me to do more. Wealth sharing would eradicate a lot of the world's problems. We wouldn't have disease, global warming or landfill, we'd be looking at a whole different earth for our kids."

PAYAL KOTHARI AT HER HOME IN MUMBAI, INDIA.

# THE FUTURE OF MONEY AND BUSINESS

The Sharing Economy is known as the biggest business trend of all time and the meteoric rise of businesses like Airbnb, now valued in billions, has shaken industries, cities, even governments. Whole markets have been disrupted, with hundred-year-old corporate monoliths displaced by companies not even a decade old. But what happens when the driving force of these Sharing Economy businesses is purely profit? How different are they from the very incumbents they set out to disrupt? If the only value they create is commercial value for themselves and their investors – where's the 'sharing' there? For despite the true breadth of the Sharing Economy, media focus has been on the Silicon Valley backed 'unicorns' that have become the poster children for this new phenomenon. This has led to a distorted perspective on what the Sharing Economy really is and the true value it creates. Inherently, that value is tripartite – economic, social and environmental – and in the future, businesses will no longer be able to focus solely on profit.

As seismic shifts happen in society and citizens have access to the resources they need, often via technology, they are increasingly no longer reliant on traditional corporations for their products, services or to live their lives. People are trading directly with each other, person-to-person, peer-to-peer, creating value for themselves, their families, their communities and the planet. Crowdfunding is a distributed form of financing and means funding a project by raising many small amounts of money from a crowd of people, usually via the internet. It's democratising finance; almost a quarter of the adult population have already participated,[84] and the sub-sector is predicted to grow to $300 billion by 2025.[85] But crowdfunding is also creating social value,

connecting communities of people (the crowd) via projects that matter to them. Alternative currencies, local currencies, crypto-currencies and blockchain are all challenging our notions of money. This alternative economy is being fuelled by micro-entrepreneurs, social entrepreneurs and agent provocateurs.

The very power structures of society are being dismantled, the control and command approaches of the past are becoming redundant. Business is far from usual and to survive, companies need to adapt and participate in the creation of social value. In the future, social and environmental considerations will drive commercial success and we are starting to see evidence of that already. Social business and social enterprise is on the rise, accounting for a quarter of new start-ups in Europe.[86] They are also at the forefront of economic recovery, outperforming their mainstream SME counterparts in nearly every area of business, from turnover growth, to job creation.[87]

**The next evolution of the Sharing Economy will see social and environmental mission supersede profit, as companies start to recognise that in future, the only way to achieve commercial success is to create community and planetary wealth too. The Davids who unseated the Goliaths are being brought to task by a new generation of social entrepreneurs who know that value needs to, and will be, shared.**

LENA LIBRARY WINDOW, AMSTERDAM.

# THE SHARING ECONOMY BUSINESS EXPERT

**Clare Kandola** is 44 years old and from the UK. At charity *The People Who Share*, she gets mainstream organisations and start-ups future-ready by helping them to create social and environmental value by participating in the Sharing Economy.

" I spent years working in corporates, dissatisfied by the inflexibility and missed opportunity of businesses, where profit was the sole objective. There was a chance to bring together Sharing Economy knowledge and business experience, to enable organisations of different sizes to succeed. We are at the end of cheap, easily available resources. The Sharing Economy is about sustainable futures and offers an opportunity for organisations to rethink their structure, relationships with their workers, investors, partners and competitors to grow into the future. That means finding other definitions of value and corporate objectives.

I question any organisation that does not have some interest in sustainability and social impact in a world of diminishing resources and greater inequality. This isn't a CSR [corporate and social responsibility] output, it's about finding ways to stay relevant and survive. Companies are increasingly impacted by the technological revolution, changing working practices and increased costs of core resources. Any organisation, in any sector, of any scale can participate in the Sharing Economy. It's just an efficient way to operate, it has social and environmental value and companies are financially more sustainable.

We are seeing a shift in consumer expectations. Now it is the voice of the crowd that matters with reputation and trust as key currencies. The crowd co-creates products and services, provides a customer base, and ensures that the business remains relevant. Taking your organisation on a journey to become a more values-driven, cooperating structure is where we step in. We highlight how the value sits within your crowd, how to reach that crowd, and enable the organisation to grow sustainably.

In the future, collaboration, partnership and the ability to work with others in a non-hierarchical, open-source way will be essential. The traditional control and command structure of a business will disappear and horizontal structures will replace them.

There has to be a shift in focus to 'tripartite value', with all value being recognised as the wealth underpinning our economy. These values need to be enshrined in the corporate culture and those who can see the opportunity, who share the effort to support more than just a bottom line, will survive and thrive. The payback of sharing and investing now is that you will not only perform well in the future but you will also have built a strong community and contributed to a healthier, more sustained society. "

CLARE KANDOLA, SHARING ECONOMY CONSULTANT, LONDON, UK.

# THE TRANSPARENT SHARER

**Carla Murphy** is the 43-year-old Chief Brand and Product Officer for New Zealand based apparel brand, icebreaker.[88] icebreaker creates natural-fibre based apparel, as the alternative to plastic-based synthetics. The company challenges the status quo of the apparel industry, championing transparent, sustainable and responsible ways to do business.

**"Transparency builds trust, relationships and can drive change through collaboration. Transparency is not about perfection, it's about sharing progress, sharing the work still to be done and sharing new ways of doing things. It is knowledge that can enable new conversations and those conversations can be the sparks that propel us forward, driving new industry behaviours, standards and enabling a brighter, more sustainable future for us and for generations to come.**

The human-generated impact on the geological landscape is now reaching epic proportions and many geologists argue we are moving into the age of the human-centric Anthropocene. This geological shift began in the mid-twentieth century when new industries developed fast, nuclear chemicals were tested and consumerism sky-rocketed, promoting the fascination with fast, plastic-driven, accessible, throwaway goods, often without the small print explaining how things were made and what the implication of those choices had on us and the planet.

I made the choice to seek out a role within a purpose-led company, with a mission to challenge the status quo and drive industry change around how apparel businesses source, make, communicate and act.

Transparency for icebreaker is inherent, it's in our DNA. We believe nature has the answers. Making clothing inspired by nature is important to us, but how we do that is central to our purpose. We do it with integrity, transparency, responsibility and care for our employees, partners and customers. When people know how products are made and their impact, they have the ability to make different choices.

I'm passionate about changing the conversation from what you wear, to why you wear it. It's become the norm to understand organics and natural alternatives in foods and skincare, yet in apparel it's a non-conversation. As the second biggest pollutant of the planet, the apparel industry has to change and fast, but I'm optimistic that in times of crisis, innovation and creativity is at its best. Awareness is rising, but not quick enough, we need to keep sharing what we know, and being transparent about how clothes are made to drive a different outcome.

**As humans we might not be able to reverse the damage to the planet, but we have the potential to reduce our impact by seeking out new alternatives and more circular and sustainable ways of doing business. The future of business needs to be smarter, more collaborative and agile. By working together, we are better and the apparel industry as a unit will be able to re-set its future."**

(L TO R) ICEBREAKER GROWERS CLASSING THE MERINO WOOL; CARLA MURPHY; MERINO WOOL TOPS AT CHARGEURS FACTORY; LINDIS PEAK STATION, NEW ZEALAND.

# THE WELLBEING ECONOMIST

Larch Maxey is 43 years old and is the Community Projects Manager at the *Network of Wellbeing*, a charity that works to ensure the wellbeing of people within the planet's natural limits.

"Research shows that if inequality goes up, wellbeing goes down. So sharing is a great way to help bring about a more equal society, which is better for our wellbeing.

Wealth for me encompasses all aspects of life; it includes money and assets, but it also includes the quality of relationships, with ourselves, our environment and the wider world. Money is a form of energy, a useful tool which should serve us, rather than something we become a slave to. The economy, like money, is a tool to help us achieve things that matter and shouldn't rule us; it requires all these currencies of care, compassion and community in order to exist and function.

GDP is a tool which has become overused and given too much power in shaping policies and ideas. Simon Kuznets developed GDP as we know it and was clear that it should be used as an emergency wartime measure, not in the blanket way it is today, due to its many limitations. The Network of Wellbeing are helping the shift away from GDP and towards wellbeing measures of value. Wellbeing measures are based on what people value and over 40 years of research. Measures such as the number and strength of our relationships, levels of fairness and justice, the richness of our lives and that of the natural world and our culture tell us far more about our true value.

Our current financial system is based on outdated models and world views such as competition versus cooperation. Both occur and are 'needed' to some extent, but research shows we are all better off if we emphasise cooperation, equality, fairness and sharing. It's fiction to assume that we need economic growth to improve wellbeing. I'd like to see an economy which empowers people, promotes personal, social and environmental wellbeing above all else."

LARCH MAXEY, TOTNES, UK.

# THE POST-CAPITALIST ENTREPRENEUR

**Boyd Cohen**, PhD, is 46 years old and from the USA. He is the Dean of Research at the EADA Business School in Barcelona and the author of *Post-Capitalist Entrepreneurship*.

❝ There are a lot of business students who think purely about profit; I'm trying to impact them to think differently. With Sharing Economy business models, you have both platform capitalism and platform cooperatism. Platform capitalism takes a market-based, profit-driven approach. A platform cooperative takes a commons-based approach and is designed to sell a service or product that is collectively owned and governed by the people who depend on and participate in it.

My research shows that capitalism is a flawed mechanism for economic exchange and needs replacing. I'm using 'post-capitalist entrepreneurship' to create a scalable, cooperative platform model for mobility. We are facilitating the creation of a new platform cooperative economy, using blockchain technology and bitcoin. In this new economy, if you want to create a taxi cooperative, we are building open source, scalable technology that any platform cooperative in the world could use. There are a lot of local taxi platform cooperatives, and if we want to compete with platform monopolies like Uber but bring value to all, we have to have scalable technology and be part of a global network without the owner of the profits dictating how much money you charge.

We need a radical rethink if we want to sustain and improve life on earth for our children. Our education system is totally messed up. We are training our youth to get jobs in companies, yet between AI, big data, robots and automation there aren't even going to be jobs in companies in the future. So we need to promote Sharing alternatives. We need to think about a future without work the way we historically define it. Taking care of an elderly person or a sick mother is a different kind of work that society doesn't value, yet it's incredibly valuable for our society. All our assumptions today are based on what you acquire is what you are worth, and the only way to own is via traditional employment. But what if our economies were connected through collaboration and alternative social currencies with basic income as part of the solution?

Through collaboration, my goal is that we would collectively achieve the creation, growth and dominance of an alternative economic model globally, which is focused on sharing, equality and environmental responsibility – a worldwide ecosystem of local, regional and global players. I'm working with others to make it a reality. ❞

BOYD COHEN, BARCELONA, SPAIN.

SHARE AND SHARE ALIKE: (L TO R) VARDA LIVNE, AMOS DAVIDOWITZ, BATYA GREENMAN, RABBI STEVE BURNSTEIN, LISA STEIN, ARIE BRAUDE, KIBBUTZ GEZER, ISRAEL.

# IS SHARING CULTURAL?

> **"Whether it is how you bring up your children, or how you come together over a meal, culture is all about sharing. If we can remind people of that, tap into that, then we're onto something."**
>
> **Shaff Prabatani, Sharer, UK**

> **"Through inter-cultural sharing, we are able to learn and understand different cultures and the diversity of humanity."**
>
> **Ji Hae Kim, Sharer, South Korea**

The different meanings of the word 'culture' demonstrate that it is inextricably linked to Sharing. One can't exist without the other. Whether culture means the arts and other expressions of 'human intellectual achievement regarded collectively' or 'the ideas, customs and social behaviour of a particular people or society' (for example 'Jewish culture'), Sharing is intrinsic. Perhaps, as social psychologist Geert Hofstede suggested, culture is either stuff made by humans (music, painting, folklore...) or 'software of the mind', a collective phenomenon shared with people who live in the same environment. Arguably, any culture is a system of shared meanings; it can't exist in isolation, it's a way of thinking, feeling and knowing about the world.[89] It's a shared 'web of significance that we have spun for ourselves'.[90]

So do different religions, regions and communities view Sharing contrarily? When it comes to Sharing, do they have and practice different cultural norms? Are some societies more sharing than others? In a Sharing world, our cultural norms, traditions and creative activities root themselves in collaboration, cooperation and community. This is an ecosphere far away from inequality, poverty and hyper consumption. For a Sharing culture to be mainstream, a significant shift is required. It's about changing our value system, from me to we, from consumer to user and from owner to co-operator. In a Sharing society, sustainability supersedes selfishness and inclusivity is vital, as Ghandi said, 'No culture can live if it attempts to be exclusive.'

Culture could be considered as the foundation of sustainability. A Sharing civilisation that is built on the values of justice, equity and solidarity, whose ultimate purpose is to achieve individual, social and environmental durability, would need new social organisations, economic models and new forms of collaboration between individuals and community, public and private. Perhaps what's needed is 'a new economy of culture'?[91]

Though Sharing isn't mainstream yet, our *Generation Share* stories show that people are leading lives based on Sharing principles and they're contributing to a shared culture, a future for humanity. They see Sharing as fundamental to our evolution; that collectively we can achieve all we need to. They understand that 'the revolution requires new cultures, new social organisations and new economic models,'[92] and that this one will certainly be digitised. As Edgar Morin[93] asserts, 'The world requires the collective building of new ways of perceiving, thinking, acting and an equal, dignified citizenship to all human beings.'

But it's not just about developing the new, it's also about re-discovering our Sharing traditions that have existed for millennia. By combining them with new ways of thinking, new technologies, new 'software of the mind', the result is a society where we are collaborative citizens, we all contribute, we all gain and it's win-win for the culture of humanity.

# THE KIBBUTZNIK

**Amos Davidowitz** is a 59-year-old leader and activist in the kibbutz movement. He is one of *Kibbutz Gezer*'s 350 residents and has lived there since 1984.

" Kibbutz is an intentional society built to redefine the economic and social relationships of people, to create a collective culture that is connected to the land, its cycles and rhythms. It served an important structural purpose in the early stages of the establishment of the state of Israel. Back then, the kibbutz provided food for the general population, housing for refugees and security for everyone.

In the early kibbutz, people literally did not own their underwear, even the children were seen as 'Children of the Kibbutz', some went so far as deciding on the name of the child communally. Your day was not yours, your work was decided by the kibbutz. Now most of the sharing is done on a voluntary basis. It could be using someone's house for visitors when the family is gone, sharing tools or knowledge. When there is a tragedy, the whole community gets together to assist. When a child is born there is a rotation of cooking to help the new parents. If you compare it to a society outside kibbutz, it is still very sharing.

There is a resurgence of a will to do things mutually. Our kibbutz is a green kibbutz, so there's a very high awareness of ecology with many communal projects, because you need a bunch of people to plant a large edible garden.

A lot of people who grew up on kibbutz are part of the social changes happening in Israel. Even those who run large corporations carry the values of the kibbutz. One of the vice presidents of Converse, when interviewed because of their relatively progressive conditions in how they treat people, said – 'I grew up on a kibbutz'. The founder of We Work used to live on a kibbutz, you see a number of Sharing Economy companies whose leadership grew up on kibbutz.

People still think that on kibbutz we all milk cows and share our underwear or they think it failed. Neither is correct. The fact is that there are 270 kibbutzim today that managed to go through radical changes and flourish. It is a very resilient form of cooperation and living. Today, we are hearing many voices seeking community and an escape from the stifling urban life. Kibbutz offers that. The future of kibbutz seems very bright to me, as people seek a healthy community and lifestyle. "

AMOS DAVIDOWITZ (MIDDLE) WITH DADS AND GRANDADS COLLECTING THEIR CHILDREN FROM THE MISMESH BABY HOUSE; RECYCLING AREA; CLOTHING HUB, KIBBUTZ GEZER, ISRAEL.

# THE OPEN KITCHEN

**Kamaljit Singh** is 25 years old and belongs to the *Shri Damesh Darbar Gurdwara*, a Sikh temple in Mumbai. Like all Gurdwaras, they run an open kitchen called a *langar*, where anyone of any age, religion, gender and economic background can come any day of the week and enjoy a free meal. The Gurdwara feeds 100–150 people every day.

" The *langar* is a practice which was started by our first guru to eliminate caste discrimination. You can see the king and the beggar sitting next to each other, eating the same quantity of food, from the same kind of plate. Anyone, from any religion can come to eat here, Hindus, Muslims, Jains. The purpose of the *langar* is to share, help and serve humanity.

It is open 24/7. You can go to any *gurdwara* and if food isn't being served at that time, you can ask for it. In the Sikh religion, we believe in sharing. Every Sikh is supposed to give 10% of their income to help the poor and needy. We believe it is only by sharing that you will spread happiness. Sharing can solve the problems of castism, racism and prejudice, because everyone is treated equally, it is the right thing to do. If I go to my office and I have food but my colleague does not, then I should share my food.

Here at the *gurdwara*, we have volunteers from the community who come and do *seva* or 'selfless service', which could be anything from cutting up bread to washing dishes. People do this to get blessings from the guru. Every day we have homeless people who come here, stand in line and receive food. In the evenings when I come here to do my *seva*, it feels good, after a day at the office, to share. It makes me feel emotional because I can see the good that sharing brings to others. "

EAT, PRAY, SHARE: (LEFT PAGE), COMMUNAL EATING AT THE LANGAR, (TOP) KAMALJIT PRAYING, (MIDDLE) SHARED KITCHEN, (BOTTOM) COOKING CHAPATIS, SHRI DAMESH DABAR GURDWARA, MUMBAI, INDIA.

# SHARING THROUGH RELIGION

**Susan Kabani** is 34 years old and a Shia Muslim from Chicago. She's also the founder of *Ugenie*, a platform that enables organisations to share knowledge effectively with their community.

" A lot of my sharing is down to upbringing and how much time I spent in my community – that's what has shaped me. In my congregation, which is about 600 people, my parents were part of the leadership when I was young. I was raised by the volunteers in the community centre, just as much as my parents. I had a lot of role models and so that's where I got into sharing.

One of the guiding principles of my faith is generosity. That generosity can be demonstrated in so many ways, but fundamentally, you can share time, money or resources. It is not just a practice, it's a way of life, it's embedded in our faith. One of the reasons we fast is to acknowledge that not everybody has everything that we have in the West, not everyone can go and get food from the fridge and not think twice about it. There is a huge connection between the fundamental tenets of religion and sharing.

In the West, everyone is more individualistic. It is all about my car, my time, my life and not as much about 'we'. There is a huge cultural difference in sharing and how we see these things. So, the further east you go, there is more sharing. My immediate family has 200 people, my mother has seven elder brothers and sisters, so inevitably we share food, clothes and responsibilities.

I started Ugenie because I realised that I could use technology to allow people to share more, to recreate that community of my childhood. I decided to see how I could create a platform for organisations to share content and knowledge efficiently. The aim is to allow people to share across communities, to bring people of different communities, faiths and socioeconomic backgrounds together. "

SUSAN KABANI, FOUNDER OF UGENIE, CENTRAL LONDON, UK.

# THE INCLUSIVE SHARER

**Shaff Prabatani** is 47 years old and from London. He is a social inclusion worker and the founder of *Storemates*, a Sharing platform that enables people from low-income backgrounds to access extra space to store their belongings.

"Sharing and inclusivity are two sides of the same coin. Exclusivity means you have a right or privilege for something in life. Unfortunately, we do not live in a meritocratic society and not many people have opportunities. Sharing is a way to allow excluded communities to have opportunities. It opens doors and helps people feel included so that they can share something. Every community, every child, every family I see, has a lot of potential to be a better person and contribute to society. The things that hold them back are lack of opportunities, lack of resources, lack of space or exclusion. As a child I saw people around me protesting about social issues and I would always think, 'What can I do to contribute and improve society?'

I am a second-generation immigrant and when I listen to stories about Africa, my family felt they were affluent. They only had one bicycle between them but they just knew how to borrow and it was completely normal to them. There was no need to own everything. It is access not ownership that will enable you to get more out of your life. Embedding that culture through trust, through platforms and making it accessible – sharing can do so much.

We need a culture shift and for a lot of people, in low-income communities who've been sold the idea of consuming stuff, sharing is difficult, because it involves giving up 'prize items' that are seen as trophies. It is about becoming a society where you share first before you consume. It's about going back to who we really are. I would like everybody, by default, to think, 'What can I give? What can I share?' Ask that first before you buy anything. Ultimately, sharing is embedded in all cultures. It is deeply rooted. Whether it is how you bring up your children or how you come together over a meal, culture is all about sharing. If we can remind people of that, tap into that, then we're onto something."

SHAFF PRABATANI; FILM WORKSHOP FOR ADULTS WITH LEARNING DIFFICULTIES, STOWE COMMUNITY CENTRE, LONDON, UK.

# THE COMMUNITY SHARERS

Cathelijn de Reede (33) and Mischa Woutersen (33) are from the Netherlands and run the *Benches Collective*, a community initiative where people put benches outside their homes to bring people together. They organise an annual event known as the 'largest open-air café', where people can register their bench locations on a map and find others nearby. There are now over 1,200 registered, customised and shared 'benches' worldwide, hosting everything from clothes swaps to salsa classes or simply a place to enjoy a cup of coffee.

**Cathelijn:** My friends Jesse, Jos and I realised that simply by putting a bench outside your home, it attracted people to stop, sit and chat. I had been living in the same area for ten years and knew my immediate neighbours, but not others down the street. By putting out a bench, I got to know people with different incomes, religious backgrounds and cultures. The benches get used every day and become meeting places. You see people drinking coffee or enjoying a moment in the sun. It's thinking of the pavement as a shared living room.

**Mischa:** It's about becoming less anonymous, making more contact and creating more understanding between each other. Often today, people are on social networks all the time and the benches are a good way for them to meet in real life, to deal with loneliness, to break down social barriers.

**Cathelijn:** We did some research about the impact of the benches and people said that by getting to know their neighbours, they feel safer and more at home in their neighbourhood. It's the idea that you feel at home even before you turn your key in the lock. 64% of people said they see each other regularly after meeting at the benches, and some figured out new ways to improve their neighbourhood. So, it also acts a kick-starter for developing a more sharing, community culture.

**Mischa:** People at the subway stop started saying 'Hi' to each other, someone met their babysitter at a bench and someone else found a musician to play in their band.

**Cathelijn:** There is a lot of diversity in neighbourhoods, but that alone does not kick-start a conversation, you need another catalyst for that. To create a more sharing, connected culture, we need to show that public spaces are for the public. Our goal is to make that happen, to celebrate this way of connecting.

THE BENCHES COLLECTIVE: (L TO R) LEAH SHAFFER, CATHELIJN DE REEDE, SEAN RYS AND MISCHA WOUTERSEN, DE CEUVEL, SUSTAINABILITY AND CULTURAL INNOVATION ZONE, AMSTERDAM.

# THE DIVERSITY SHARER

**Samantha Williams** is 42 years old and from Barbados. She is the founder of *Book Love*, a Sharing business that promotes culturally diverse children's books.

" There is a real under-representation of black and minority children in children's books. If you go to any high street bookshop or your school library, nine times out of ten, the characters and the protagonists are white, blond, blue-eyed princesses. These are the images that black children, minority children and white children are looking to, so it's a warped view of the world. In my children's school there are over 70 languages spoken, but you pick up the books that they are reading and there is no one that looks like them. There are no children wearing hijabs, no boys with dreadlocks, no girls with Afros, so why would they want to read them?

I've developed Book Love as a sharing concept and a business concept. I go to schools, people's homes and book fairs. I ask any family that walks by, 'How many children's books do you have with a character that isn't white?' Usually the answer is 'None' and straight away you make them think, then they buy a book and take their child into another world.

To know that children are taking these books home and feeling more positive about themselves because they are seeing themselves represented is priceless. A lot of girls want to have straight hair because they look in traditional story books and the pretty girls have straight hair. They believe this is what beautiful looks like, so they don't want an Afro. A lot of the mums say 'We sit down and we read the stories together and she is learning to love herself, she is celebrating her curls.'

Most of these books are self-published, written by people who are holding down a full-time job. So I'm finding new authors and sharing their stories with a wider audience. Publishing companies aren't interested in books that have a black child on the front or an Asian child with a headscarf. These writers are telling their own uncensored, authentic stories about their community and both the authors and illustrators are getting an opportunity to showcase their work. We're doing this among ourselves, because if the publishing companies aren't going to do it, we're going do it. "

SAMANTHA WILLIAMS AT HOME IN SOUTH LONDON, UK.

# THE INTER-CULTURAL SHARER

**"** Through inter-cultural sharing, I started to make bonds with people from different communities, so rather than living in another country and being with an exclusively Korean community, I was able to get to know people from other cultures and understand the diversity of humanity. **"**

**Ji Hae Kim, participant in ALCE (Appetite for Learning Comes with Eating) intercultural Sharing project**

JI HAE KIM (37) FROM SEOUL, SOUTH KOREA, PARTICIPANT IN ALCE (APPETITE FOR LEARNING COMES WITH EATING), INTERCULTURAL SHARING PROJECT, PANTIN, FRANCE.

# THE WORKERS' CAFÉ

**Mike Sylvester** is 30 years old and from London. He runs the *Workers' Café*, a community co-working café in Dalston.

❝ A lot of the time, you find freelancers in cafés but it is not the most ideal place for them to be because cafés can get expensive. Here, we have designed a co-working café for the community and it is okay if workers spend the whole day here. We've created a place where they come in and meet other like-minded people and build friendships and networks. They also share knowledge and information.

Everyone helps each other out and it is free. This is a nice way for freelancers to cultivate a sense of community. It instils trust and brings people together. There's a culture of sharing, and that's what builds communities. People hang out and talk and meet up outside the space as well.

The Workers' Café attracts creative-minded people, freelancers and remote workers. They say it feels like a home away from home yet, they are not distracted by Netflix or the dog and it feels comfortable, it is their space. It is very local; some people literally live two doors down. They say they can get a lot more work done because they are around other people that are working. Sharing is intrinsic to building a healthy community culture. ❞

MIKE SYLVESTER; HANGING OUT; COFFEE TIME, WORKERS' CAFE, DALSTON, LONDON, UK.

# THE LAUGHTER SHARER

Comedienne Natasha Wood is 48 years old and from the UK. She challenges stereotypes by sharing laughter in her daily interactions and through performance. Her autobiographical, bawdy one-woman show, *Rolling with Laughter*, about living with rare muscular disease Spinal Muscular Atrophy was a hit in the UK and Hollywood.

**"It's always been about sharing laughter for me. My dad taught me a great lesson as a kid, to always use humour. Being a market trader, you don't get much more sharing than being a market trader, we'd have such a laugh. I was a gobby little girl, selling knickers and bras on a market stall, bolted in a brace, I couldn't move my head, all I could move was my eyes, I'd look up and go, 'Can I help you love? You're a 36B!' All I wanted to do was make people laugh.**

Sharing humour is the only way for me. I did a speaking session with a group of disabled teenagers and one of the 17 year olds said, 'If you could give me one piece of advice, what would that be?' I said, 'Always laugh and use humour.' These kids were teased in school and going through tough times. He said, 'Give me an example.' I said, 'I was flying to LA with a friend – not a carer – and an older man comes to assist me, to put me on the plane and says to my friend – not to me and I'm right there – 'Right then, so she's the one I've got to put on the plane, what do I have to think about?' and I go, 'Great, so you are the sexy young man who will be putting me on the plane, phwoar! I like the look of you!'

So, we spent an hour with him, he put me in the first class lounge and we laughed and laughed. The truth is, it was his job to put me on the plane and I could have said to him, 'Are you for real mate? I'm down here and I'm a person, so you can speak to me.' But where would that have got me? He went home and it was his birthday and I told him he needed to get home with nothing on but a tie – stick to the birthday suit and tell his missus what to do to him. My friend said to me, 'You've just completely changed his perception, his job was to put disabled people on the plane every day and you've changed the way he sees disabled people.' He probably went home and said to his missus, 'I had this woman today, she was hilarious, oh yeah, and she was in a wheelchair.' That's why sharing laughter means so much to me, because with humour, you see the person and not the disability. If you share a smile in the street, you see the difference that makes to the other person. I try now not to ever have my head down, it's so much better to look up and smile. I like to see comedy in everything. The best thing you can do every day is to make someone laugh, share the laughter. **"**

AT HOME WITH NATASHA WOOD, NOTTINGHAM, UK.

# THE COMMUNITY CHOIR

" When we sing together, we share something more than just that magic time for ourselves and our wellbeing... we literally share harmonic vibrations in our bodies as our voices blend. It's a true and tangible sense of feeling united and powerful in this increasingly polarised and lonely world. There's no other feeling like it, we become better connected to ourselves and the community around us; this joy we find in singing together has a ripple effect. "

**Sarah Tohill, choir starter, The Dulcetones community choir**

CHOIR STARTER SARAH TOHILL (34) WITH THE DULCETONES COMMUNITY CHOIR, LATEST MUSIC BAR, BRIGHTON, UK.

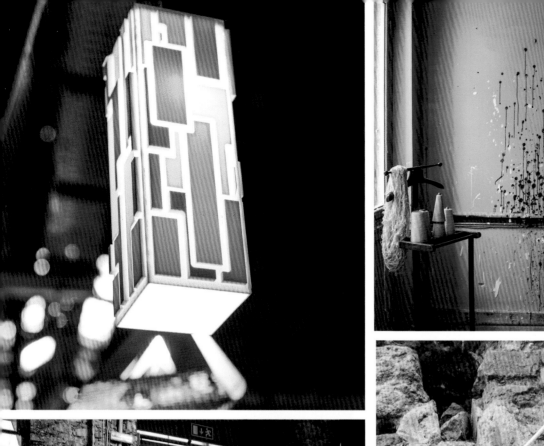

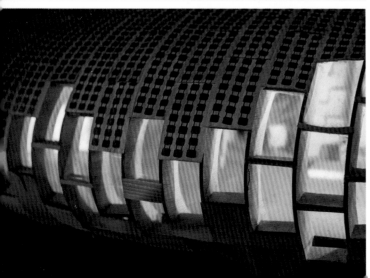

# CREATIVITY AND THE MAKER MOVEMENT

"**M**ore than mere consumers of technology, we are makers, adapting technology to our needs and integrating it into our lives. Some of us are born makers and others, like me, become makers almost without realising it.**"**

When tech writer Dale Dougherty opened his column in the premiere issue of *Make* magazine, in February 2005, he had no idea that he would ignite a worldwide community of independent inventors, designers, tinkerers, artisans, hackers and DIY-ers and spark a global movement. Twenty-two thousand enthusiasts turned up for the first Maker Faire at a suburban fairground in San Francisco in 2006; 13 years later, that number has swelled to over 135 million.[94]

With more than 1,200 Fab Labs in over 100 countries, the growth of the movement is due to a feeling of disconnection from the physical world and a desire to experiment and co-create: 'As human beings, from infancy we learn about the world by manipulating it, by sort of poking it and seeing how it pokes back.'[95]

Propelled by technology, these fabricators have democratised invention. Empowered to design, co-create and share their open-source products and prototypes, the Maker Movement has sparked what Neil Gershenfeld called 'the next digital revolution', which put 'the means of fabrication on people's desks'. Affordable digital tools such as 3D printers and laser cutters, made available in Makerspaces and Fab Labs, alongside traditional wood and metalworking instruments, have attracted a global community of change-makers to reimagine homes, cities and the world at large.

The community is at once manufacturer, lab, tech campus and system innovator, yet none of this could work without sharing. Indeed, makers are usually more passionate about collaborating than going solo. It is in this Fab(rication) revolution that Fab(ulous), shared creativity happens, free from the constraints of mass production and markets.

(TOP LEFT) FAB LAB BARCELONA; (MIDDLE) REPAIR CAFE AT ORGANII ECO MARKET, LXFACTORY; (BOTTOM) FAB LAB; (TOP RIGHT) COMMUNITISM, ATHENS; (BOTTOM) FAB LAB BARCELONA.

COMMUNITISM PROJECT, KARAMEIKOU, ATHENS, GREECE.

# THE ARTISTIC SHARER

**Natasha Dourida is 33 years old and from Athens. She set up *Communitism*, a self-funded socio-cultural project, which brings together groups of artists and creative people from different cultural backgrounds to overcome differences and rebuild society.**

" I have this vision of a city and its culture, managed and reimagined by communities. We bring together different creative communities through a series of events held in heritage buildings. By coming to share our creativity, we are able to reconnect with our heritage, bring abandoned buildings back to life and give them a renewed cultural significance.

This project is about looking around us, and despite all the economic, social and environmental challenges, we find ways to share common sense, we get away from our own egos, our prejudices and really look at the person who is next to us, regardless of which culture they are from. Once we do that we can find ways to help each other and communicate what we have in common.

The idea is to create a home for everyone who wants to be a part of this new community. While we rebuild these walls, we start to bring down the social and cultural walls that create tensions between different people. The most important aspect is the people, not the buildings themselves, it's the creativity, the humanity, the knowledge that people bring to create a shared culture. We are creating a new, shared, cultural heritage for Greece – one that is worth celebrating. By co-creating this together, the end result belongs to all of us. "

COMMUNITISM: NATASHA
DOURIDA, KARAMEIKOU 28,
ATHENS, GREECE.

# THE MAKER

**Ricardo Valbuena is a 33-year-old Maker from Mexico. He works in *Fab Labs*, creative spaces where anyone can 'fabricate'.**

"Fab Lab started as an initiative to change our mass production and consumption culture. Fab Labs give tools and power to people, so that they can make conscious decisions about what they are buying, using, wasting and instead create and transform things. Anyone can become a Maker; you can learn how to use the machinery, you can customise items, be part of the process, even change the materials entirely. A Maker culture means that by being part of the creative process, you connect more with the things that you use. It's a way to reach zero waste, to create a circular, more sharing economy.

The Maker Movement is based on the concept of open source, sharing knowledge, sharing software, sharing ideas and putting it on the internet for everyone to benefit from and contribute to. It means that rather than creating a design and owning it, you share it and others can use it in a different country or context, so ideas can reach a global audience and many can benefit. It's a type of creative, cultural transformation that puts people and planet first. I believe this is our future culture. "

RICARDO VALBUENA, FAB LAB, BARCELONA.

# THE FAB CAFÉ

**Barbara Andreatta** is **34** years old and from Italy. She runs the *FabCafe* in Barcelona, an open space where people can access digital fabrication tools, such as **3D** printers and bring their digital data to life. *FabCafe Barcelona* is part of a global network that started in Taipei, Taiwan in 2013.

" The idea of FabCafe is to make digital technologies and programming available to everyone. When you have a digital fabrication machine, a 3D printer and a laser in an open space in a coffee shop, people come in to get their coffee and discover that you don't have to be Superman or Wonder Woman to use them. We make it normal for people to be creative; a 3D printer is just a small machine that melts plastic. You have permission here to make mistakes, we share our mistakes, it's how you learn.

I'm a 'community gardener', which means that I take care of the whole space. For me, community is the foundation of any kind of initiative because without people you can't do anything. It doesn't matter what your qualifications are, you are so much more than your CV. People can do a lot more together than by themselves. Recently, there was a guy whose mum had a birthday and another guy helped him create the perfect birthday card for her. So it is not just about selling products, it is about being human.

'Fabing' is all about sharing, it's about being part of an ecosystem, working with others to build upon ideas, to improve them, to innovate. We have a program called Fab Master that is trying to fill in the gap between formal education and new technologies. We want to democratise the digital fabrication movement by sharing knowledge. All our classes are free, it's very geeky, but anyone can do it! In the future, I'd like to see lots of initiatives like this. Programming is the language of the future. People will learn Spanish, Italian, English and, say, 'Java!' 💬

**❝ I just discovered the FabCafe while travelling in Barcelona. I had never heard of 'fabing' before. I spotted this on the street and love the fact that I can drink coffee, share my designs and print them on a 3D printer! ❞**

**Irina Marcopol (27), from Romania, FabCafe, Barcelona**

(L TO R) BARBARA ANDREATTA AND CRISTINA CÁRDENAS, FABCAFE; IRINA MARCOPOL (27), FABCAFE, BARCELONA.

HOVE PROMENADE, UK.

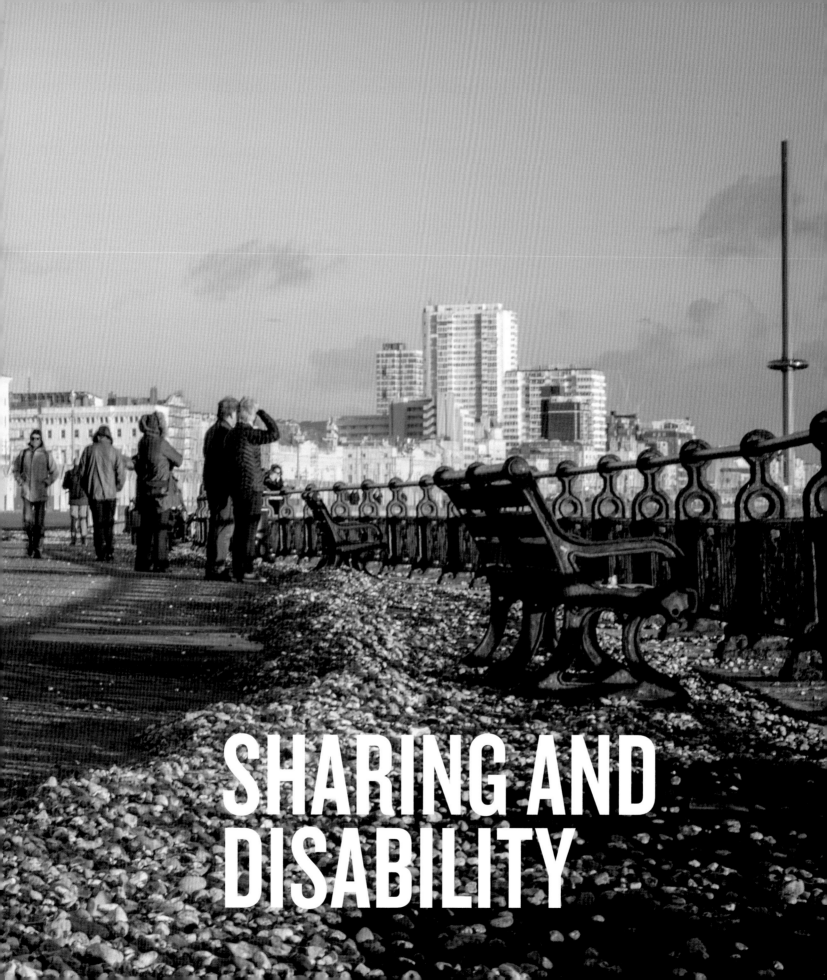

# SHARING AND
# DISABILITY

> **"One thing that's nice about being disabled is that it makes you aware of your own dependence on other people. I can't get dressed, go to the toilet or eat without assistance. Of course, no one else can either, right? We invisibilise the sewage worker, we invisibilise the people who make the clothes, they are somewhere else, but your dependence on them is enormous. Sharing is just very visible when you're disabled."**

**Jacob Berkson, founder, Thousand 4 £1000**

For Jacob Berkson, a 36-year-old campaigner for migrant rights, Sharing is an all too pertinent subject. Following a severe spinal cord injury at the age of 21, he has to share his daily life with a carer who helps him with his basic needs. He believes that we all share every single day, we just might not know it. Indeed, this 'invisible sharing' is precisely what his campaigning group, *Thousand 4 £1000*, which crowdfunds rent for refugees, seeks to make visible to the wider public.

In November 2017, disability activist Annie Segarra started a Twitter campaign using the hashtag #InvisiblyDisabledLooksLike to mark the end of *Invisible Disabilities Week*. She invited people to share their photos, to challenge perceptions and make their stories known. Seventy-four per cent of people with disabilities do not use a wheelchair or anything that might visually signal their disability[96] and about 1 in 5 people worldwide are disabled. Less likely to find employment due to discrimination, people with disabilities are twice as likely to live in poverty.[97]

The Sharing Economy helps to bring 'visibility' to the 'invisible', enabling an understanding that our biases (conscious or unconscious) lead to discrimination and inequality. But it's also about understanding that, as Jacob Berkson suggests, none of us could lead our lives without the hidden sharing that happens continually.

When we make assumptions based on biases and exclude others by engaging in non-sharing behaviour, we contribute to the problem. It's by making evident and understanding these connections (like car use and consumption leads to pollution, poverty and homelessness), by 'internalising our externalities', that we can start to build a truly transparent Sharing Economy, where everything is counted, connected and seen; where the impact of our actions or inactions are understood.

Sharing Economy platforms and technology make it easier for disabled people to get around cities and access employment, goods or services. Blind customers find hailing a ride simpler, since payments are handled via an app, and they do not have to worry about overcharging.[98] Sharing services are found to be reliable, with more respectful providers compared to cabs. Providers with platforms such as Lyft are more likely to open doors, help with bags and walk users to the front door. Disabled users also cite benefits such as ratings (an incentive to better customer service), along with increased choice and access to information such as photos of properties on home-sharing sites and being able to use services on demand, 24 hours a day via an app, providing greater accessibility and independence.[99]

The number of Sharing platforms offering products and services for people with disabilities is increasing. Zagster offers adaptive bikes; Wheeliz, peer-to-peer adapted car sharing; and Australia's Hireup can help users find, hire and manage support workers who share their interests. Disability home-sharing marketplace Accomable was acquired and incorporated into Airbnb to bring these offers to the mainstream. The Sharing Economy is also behind much of what's known as 'assistive tech'. Be My Eyes is a free app designed to bring 'sight' to the blind via a live video connection between blind users and sighted volunteers. Now the largest online community for the visually impaired, it helps people carry out daily tasks, from checking the sell-by date of milk, to finding your way to work. AXS Map is a crowd-sourced map with information about wheelchair-accessible ramps and toilets in public places.

Despite these offerings, a Rutgers University report found discrimination alive and well across some Sharing providers, mirroring the discrimination found in society at large. In the home-sharing arena, the pre-approval rate was 75% for travellers without disabilities, compared to 50% for travellers with blindness and 25% for those with spinal cord injury.[100] For the Sharing Economy to be truly inclusive, it too must tackle bias, cultivate diversity, create good jobs and focus on human-centred design at a system level. Communities, leaders and CEOs need to take responsibility by shaping organisational culture and making inclusion a priority in the media, in homes, schools and the investment sphere. It is only then that the Sharing Economy can help make the invisible visible.

# CROWDFUNDING FOR REFUGEES

**Jacob Berkson** is **36 years old and is from the UK. He set up** *Thousand 4 £1000*, **a migrant solidarity campaign that crowdfunds rent for refugees in Brighton.**

"We crowdfund rent though reoccurring micro donations for people who are denied access to housing because of their immigration status. Some people are forced to cross borders regularly; they arrive in this country and are not entitled to work or get housing benefit, their access to housing is non-existent. It forces people into homelessness and destitution. We wanted to come together to give a little of our spare change each month. We initially said that we would get a thousand people to give us £1 a month and with £1,000 we could find a home for two people. The project has expanded beyond that.

There's a lot of sharing that happens in this work: sharing money through crowdfunding, sharing the stuff people need like bedding and vacuums, sharing space – I've usually got someone on my sofa – and sharing extraordinary quantities of time. People get excited by the project and start helping us. They meet a refugee for a cup of coffee and end up writing policies and locating insurance. It's beyond housing as they need support with their legal situation and emotional support. Often they've got kids and they are trying to look at family rights too.

We are currently housing 14 people, including two families, a mum and three kids, a family of five and three single men. It's made all the difference to their lives. One family would have been sleeping rough and their youngest is two. I've become very good friends with people who I've helped. I'm very disabled and I need care. I had a crisis – I managed to mess up the rota and I was going be without someone to help me overnight. One of our guys came to the rescue. He was able to help me. The sharing goes both ways.

In the long run we aim to be part of the dismantling of a hostile environment, so at the very least we push the border back to the border. Once you're in the country, you should have the same access to the law and goods and services as everyone else. Scaling up would create a kinder world, a world with a public space where we would be visible to each other. I want people to recognise me – I want to make a difference. I don't want us to be invisible to each other. "

TIME WELL SHARED: PILAR ESPAÑOL AND ANDREU HONZAWA, CARRER DE ROSÉS, BARCELONA, SPAIN; MARIA NIKOLOPOULOU.

# THE TIME SHARERS

Andreu Honzawa (31) and Pilar Español (59) are from Spain. They belong to *Banco de Tiempo*, a timebank in Barcelona, where people share their time in exchange for services they need. Maria Nikolopoulou (37) runs *Banco de Tiempo*, and is the secretary for the Association of Time Banking Development who have platforms across Europe and Latin America.

**Pilar:** As a blind person, I need help with everyday tasks, like going to the doctors. The timebank has made things easier for me and I've got to know a group of people in the neighbourhood that I didn't know before. It's empowering, you realise that not only can you receive help, but that you are able to help others. I offer alternative therapies like reiki and feel useful to people.

**Andreu:** When I moved to this area, I didn't know anybody, so I joined the timebank. By sharing my time, I've met so many new people by helping them. I helped someone set up a page on Wikipedia and another person move house.

**Pilar:** I like that there is a way to interact that has nothing to do with money. People have this idea that, aside from our family, everything that we give or receive has to involve money. A timebank is another way of doing things. It's a human form of exchange. Sharing time makes people equal because you give an hour and you get an hour. As a blind person, I find it empowering.

**Andreu:** Timebanking could be useful as a public policy tool. It could help refugees and others who need support. It makes people active, not passive receivers of a service.

**Maria:** Time is a tool that brings people together. It's not about getting a fee for a service. You're not putting a value on the skill, you're putting a value on the person and the time you spend with them.

**Pilar:** The timebank has helped me see the world differently – now I believe there's hope for the world.

# THE INSIGHT SHARER

Miriam Batliwala, known as 'Mimi', is 75 years old and from Mumbai. She is a Sharer of stories and the author of *InSight*, an autobiography of her life growing up as a blind person.

❝ It's important to share your story to inspire others, that's why I wrote a book about my life. If you have faith in yourself and enough courage, you are able to do anything. At the age of 12, I was diagnosed with an incurable retina disease – macular degeneration. I give credit to my mother, she never made me feel I had a problem. I had two younger siblings, and my parents just let me be like the others. They sent me to a regular school and didn't make a fuss. I had to sit in the front of the class so that I could 'see' the blackboard, which I could not see. I just got on with it.

I was in the school hockey team; I didn't consider myself as having a disability. I had my own technique, I'd follow the crowd. I figured, they are all running, the ball must be there and I would whack it. Recently, my old school friend said, 'Mimi, when you hit the ball, we'd all jump out of the way – it was hit or miss, you either got the ball or our legs!' She said I never made an issue, I refused to let my disability get in the way. I said, 'If they can play I can.'

You have to be brave. When I was working in Brussels I hid my disability. I couldn't let my colleagues know I couldn't read, otherwise I wouldn't have been allowed to do the job. I was being sent all over Europe because I spoke fluent French and Italian and was always acting. If I had to fill out a form at a hotel, I'd pretend I'd forgotten to bring my glasses and ask for help. Years later, when my colleagues read my book they couldn't believe it! I decided to write a book because people said, 'Mimi, you need to write your story down, share it.' I love that by sharing my story, people have a different perspective on disability – isn't that fantastic? I can share details of my life and that helps others.

I was asked to share my story with a group of blind kids and parents. I could feel the energy in the room was low. I said, 'Let's put on music and dance.' A couple with a seven-year-old daughter said they hadn't danced in seven years. I said, 'Do you know what you are doing to your child? She feeds off your energy.' I got them to dance and the girl's energy completely changed. This is one of the messages I share. If you have kids with disabilities, don't treat them abnormally, let them do everything. That's why I've been able to achieve all of the things I have in my life, nothing should get in your way, whether you have a physical or mental disability. If you consider yourself as normal, like everybody else, there's nothing you cannot do. ❞

# THE CHALLENGE SHARER

Sarah Burrell is 28 years old and has hemiplegia and speech dysarthria. She cannot control the right side of her body and has a speech impediment. Sarah challenges stereotypes of disability by striking up conversations with people in public places.

"Conversation is a huge aspect of sharing and meeting new people. It's important for people to recognise that being disabled doesn't mean anything other than being disabled. It doesn't mean I'm an inspiration, or that I'm anything special. It's just something that happened to me that I have to deal with every day.

I get on the tube, find someone who wants to talk and I go from there. It takes about a minute for people to adjust to my voice, then they get interested in what I'm saying. It's about sharing a story and where that might lead. Often it turns to what we both do, and a deep discussion about life in the context of inclusion; attitudes to disability and where they should be. A conversation with one person can be a drop in the ocean, but it's got one person thinking. They might share the story with others and that's how I infiltrate the wider public. It's changing mindsets, one person at a time.

Society can learn a lot from a new Sharing social model and by learning about our barriers, we create solutions. I also deliver inclusion and diversity training for companies. There's a lot of PC language and tokenism, rather than an actual ethos of being inclusive. I focus on what's actually at the heart of it, what it means to embed inclusion, true sharing and empower each other to point out unconscious bias. I help companies explore what it means to give power to everyone, not just a few, at all levels within an organisation, from interns to the CEO.

No matter how many degrees you've got, or how much work experience you gain, it's how you come across, it's the image people see. Unfortunately, I've been on the receiving end of bias for my entire career because of the way I speak and move. I've had to create my own position for myself. By sharing my approach in an honest way, I help clients not tiptoe around issues of disability, resolving rather than brushing under the carpet. Change requires people to talk about things that they feel uncomfortable with. Sharing means to actively listen to people, then you are being truly inclusive. If we can challenge the perspective, then we can move forward. "

SARAH BURRELL IN CONVERSATION WITH JUDY AJANI, DISTRICT LINE, THE TUBE, LONDON.

# THE POSITIVITY SHARER

**Elizabeth Wright** is a 38-year-old Australian Paralympic swimmer, who won bronze and silver medals at the 2000 Summer Paralympics. She runs a character education programme for children called *Resilience Wellbeing and Success* to help them achieve their potential.

"Sharing for me means positivity. I work with children to help them reach their potential and have that positive self-belief that I had as a child. I set myself the goal of winning the Paralympics when I was 13 and I wondered as an adult, what was in me that made me persevere? If I could uncover that, then I could inspire others.

When I discovered there was this thing called character, it was a light bulb moment. If we can help children develop their character and their character strengths, their ability to thrive increases. I was fortunate to have parents, teachers and coaches who believed in my ability to achieve more than doctors thought possible. We need to recognise, emphasise and celebrate a child's strengths in a positive way and build self-belief.

The kids want to have their voices and struggles heard, it's empowering for them. Today there was one boy who really struggled to think of something good that had happened in his life this week and it took a bit of discussion to draw that out. Eventually, he said, 'I got a really good mark in my spelling test and my mum was proud of me.' That's what inspires me with my work, to hear kids say these amazing things that are powerful and impactful for them.

Sharing positivity is so important. When you look at the world at the moment, there is so much doom and gloom. It's about finding the positive in small things, being grateful for what we have; even if we don't have a lot, you can still be grateful for the people in your life, or your favourite dessert.

I could spout tons of research which proves the impact of this work, it's about getting children, and not just children, to switch their thinking from the negative bias to looking for the good stuff. We all have ups and downs, it's the nature of being human, but by helping them see their lives positively, we can help them spiral upwards to thrive and flourish into the future.

If we can start to focus more on the positives and embrace that idea of sharing there'll be a lot less conflict and misunderstanding in the world. It's like ripples ... you start something, it ripples out, becomes something bigger and has a global impact, becoming a whole sharing economy. "

ELIZABETH WRIGHT WITH STUDENTS FROM BRODETSKY PRIMARY SCHOOL, LEEDS, UK.

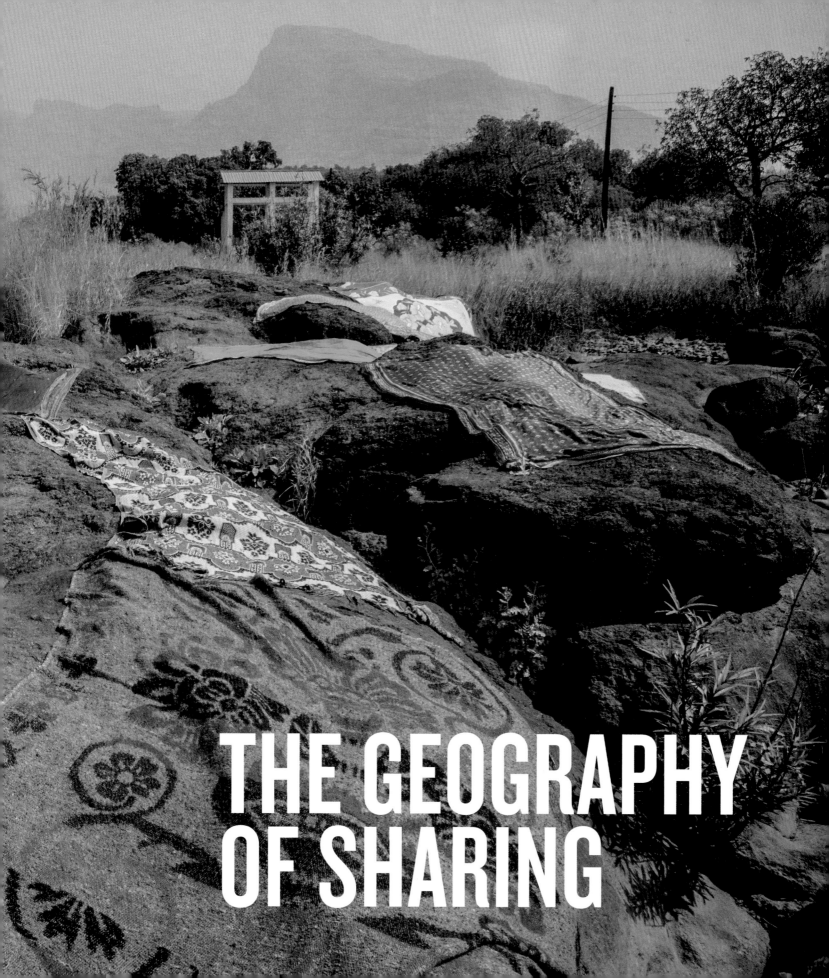

# THE GEOGRAPHY
# OF SHARING

REFURNISH VAN MAKING FREE COLLECTIONS OF REUSABLE FURNITURE, TOTNES.

Can geography have an influence on how much we share? Are some countries sanctuaries for Sharers? Is it possible to determine the most Sharing place in the world? If so, could it be New Zealand, with 75% of those moving there saying it's easy to fit in?[101] What about Norway, where the more you share, the happier you become?[102] Canada could be a good option, as personal freedom reigns there.[103] You could vote for equal Sweden, or perhaps it's positive Paraguay? While Iceland boasts the smallest gender gap,[104] maybe the strongest contender is the best country to live in – Switzerland?[105] That said, Lithuania does offer the fastest Wi-Fi, so perhaps it pips the post as the easiest place to share?[106]

Research on sharing differentiation by place is hard to come by. One study found that Asia comes out on top as the continent with the biggest appetite for Sharing, with 78% of people willing to share their own goods.[107]

To better understand the impact of place, we met, photographed and interviewed 200 people from 30 countries. Their stories are inspiring, fascinating and diverse, but three countries stood out. They encapsulated the trends, opinions and impacts that we found worldwide: the UK, Greece and India.

# SHARING: IN THE UK

When it comes to Sharing, despite our British reserve, we're a pretty forthright bunch. The UK makes up a third of all Sharing activity across Europe,[108] with 64% of us already participating in online and offline Sharing, from cars and clothes to food.[109] 80% believe Sharing makes us happy[110] and 83% say we'd share even more if it was easier.[111] This propensity to share, as history tells us, is indigenous. 1761 saw 'The Society of Weavers' set up the first cooperative organisation of the industrial age in the Ayrshire village of Fenwick. By 1831, shared ownership models proved so popular in Britain that the first national cooperative congress was held in Manchester, paving the way for the establishment of the much-celebrated 'Equitable Pioneers Co-operative Society', in Rochdale.[112]

But it's not just shared ownership that gets the Brits going. When we need to raise cash, we're partial to a collective 'whip round' – a forerunner to crowdfunding perhaps?[113] Indeed, the world's first crowdfunding project is believed to be Nelson's Column in London's Trafalgar Square, which was paid for collectively by public subscriptions in 1843.[114]

In terms of economic value, more than a million of us are already working in the UK's Sharing Economy, providing services from driving to household and creative tasks, earning billions of pounds each year[115] and making a significant contribution to GDP. By 2025, transactions in the sector could reach £140 billion, up from an estimated £13 billion predicted in 2016.[116] But what's more notable is the fact that the UK has been quick to spot the social and environmental value of Sharing, understanding that financial value only tells a small part of the story. Innovation charity Nesta launched ShareLab to grow evidence and understanding of how Sharing platforms can deliver social impact.

UnLtd, the UK's foundation for social entrepreneurs, has supported many Sharing ventures from YorSpace (cooperatively owned housing for York), the WikiHouse Foundation (sustainable, open building technologies), Migrateful (refugees sharing their cuisines and gaining employment) and Eco-communities (providing access to shared digital resources for excluded communities).

Today, the UK is seen as a global leader in the Sharing Economy and it's easy to see why. We've given birth to Global Sharing Week, created by charity The People Who Share, the largest mass engagement campaign on the Sharing phenomenon, reaching over 100 million people worldwide.[117] In keeping with our past, we've launched the world's first equity crowdfunding platform, Crowdcube. The UK is also home to Sharing trailblazers, including social business, Liftshare (which predated Facebook and Google); FareShare, who in 2018 delivered 36.7 million meals to people in poverty from food diverted from landfill;[118] and Beam, the world's first crowdfunding platform for homeless people.

Indeed, there is a tapestry of reasons for the UK's Sharing success: support for innovation, a growing social enterprise sector, strong green activism that spawned the transition town movement and a thriving technology sector. In addition, we are home to some of the world's largest charities, we have garnered political support for the Sharing Economy and it's one of the easiest places to do business. The result? The UK is at the forefront of social innovation in Sharing, worldwide.

DOG AND BONE: PHONE BOXES TURNED COMMUNITY ART GALLERY, BRIGHTON, UK.

# CROWDFUNDING FOR A FUTURE

**Alex Stephany** is 36 years old and the founder of *Beam*, the world's first crowdfunding platform that raises funds for employment training for homeless people.

**Guy** is 34 years old and from London. Locked into a life of hard drug use and homelessness, he was introduced to *Beam* and completed a crowdfunding campaign to train as an electrician.

**" Alex:** I met a homeless man on the steps of my local train station next to a stack of newspapers. He told me what it felt like to be locked out from the world and not be able to read. I wanted to take a small amount of money and make a long-term investment in his future, but I needed an organisation that could combine my £2 with your £5, and help that individual thrive. That organisation didn't exist so we started it. Beam is about making it safe and easy to help homeless people. The big vision is to unleash the talents of the more than 300,000 homeless in the UK, empowering them to 'be amazing', to make the best contribution to society and the economy. It's the collective responsibility of coming together to make a difference.

**Guy:** I've been in and out of prison, never had a stable job. I first took drugs at home with my dad when I was 10 and left school at 14, with no qualification or prospects. Turning 30 and being in a prison cell made me realise that something wasn't right. I got into a rehab programme and that brought me to Beam.

**Alex:** We're not a typical crowdfunding platform We provide two sources of value: financial and social. Donations are divided equally between members on a one-off or monthly basis. We also build a support network of people that come to the website, read someone's story and want to help. For people who have been homeless for decades, with chronic lack of self-esteem, this is transformative.

**Guy:** Three months ago, I'd never thought about becoming an electrician. I've gone from having no vision and no idea, just focusing on being clean and not using, to starting to look to the future. I've always lived in the day to day. Sharing through crowdfunding for me has meant the opportunity to share my story and get support. It's helped me to see a future for myself. I'm really grateful.

**Alex:** We're building scaffolding for people. If you have that scaffolding in place you are more likely to withstand some shocks. There are people who experience homelessness all over the world; what we are building here is globally applicable. **"**

ALEX STEPHANY, BEAM OFFICE, WEWORK LONDON; GUY, OLD STREET, LONDON, UK.

# THE STREET THAT SHARES

**Elle McAll** is **30** years old and from the **UK**. She is a creative partner at environmental charity **Hubbub** and leads a project called *The Street That Shares*. The three-year initiative is developing community sharing in four residential areas in the **UK**.

"In the UK, the impact of Brexit is causing a surge in community action to fill the policy gap. There's a spirit of 'I want to be in control' and a desire to connect with the local community. People are disillusioned with the status quo, businesses and politicians. The freeze on welfare will cost the average working family £300 a year, commodity prices have risen, people are feeling the pinch. They are having to share as a matter of necessity. People are motivated by job security and family; if sharing meets their immediate needs, then it becomes a no brainer.

The Street That Shares is about piloting and doing lots of small-scale trials in community sharing, to see what works and what doesn't, and to bring these ideas to the mainstream. We are showcasing how the community-led sharing of skills, resources and knowledge can have financial, social and environmental impacts for households. We are looking at the opportunities and the barriers; we figure out the long-term financial model and how to scale up. Once we've got those working, we open source the ideas. We've set up a network of community fridges and the ambition is to have 70 across the UK over the next 3 years. Good quality, surplus food that would otherwise be wasted can be passed on to others. They work on an honesty basis – anyone can put food in and take food out. It's also providing food for people who would not make ends meet.

Projects are developed, based on the needs of the street, so there's a lot of listening and co-creating. We are looking at community laundrettes, inspired by Sharing Economy initiatives like WeWash. Could community launderettes save money and be spaces for people to meet and learn how to make clothes last longer? We look at what has worked well internationally, which can be transferable. It's not a case of reinventing the wheel – we want to make these ideas accessible and relevant to everyone."

CATHY DREW BERESFORD (28), WITH BERTIE VIA DOG-SHARING PLATFORM, BORROW MY DOGGY, THE WAITING ROOM CAFE, BRIGHTON, UK.

# THE DOG SHARER

"I love dog sharing because both my husband and I work full-time and we travel a lot for work so we're not able to have a dog of our own. As the borrower, it's a bit like being an aunty, as people say with kids. You get to give them back at the end of the day! For the dog, they're the real winners, they get two families – so Bertie here gets all the playtime."

**Cathy Drew Beresford, dog sharer, Borrow My Doggy**

# SHARING: GOES GREEK

> **The Sharing Economy in Greece is gaining momentum because people have had to reconsider how to live and how they can make best use of resources. It's important to be able to do what you can with the resources you have.**

**Alexandros Pagidas, Sharer, Athens**

Take a walk through Athens and you're likely to find abandoned municipal buildings converted into community kitchens, parking lots transformed into performance spaces and self-managed health clinics that have past lives as cinemas. Out of the ashes of the Greek economy, a new type of bottom-up, commons-driven urbanism is emerging, one that, as Mary Valiakas believes, 'will reinstate Greece as the cradle of civilisation'. 'We've forgotten,' she says, 'that Greece gave the world democracy, philosophy and the Olympics, we're the original sharers.' With her organisation Oi Polloi (a pun on the phrase 'hoi polloi', meaning 'the masses') and a network of social organisations, Mary intends to 'reboot Greece'.

The spirit of solidarity and Sharing has captured hearts across the country since the economic crisis hit hard in 2009. People are turning to the Sharing Economy, or more accurately, 'returning to it'. They're taking their lives into their own hands because they know that the state can't. It is this combination of quasi-anarcho-community economics that is giving (or rather sharing) a future for Greece. An array of services and initiatives are popping up: an alternative currency called TEMs; Welcommon, a co-op hotel for refugees; 'live' seedbank Peliti, with its annual Olympic Seed Festival; Habibi.Works, a Fab Lab based at the refugee camp of Katsikas; and EasyBike, the first Greek bike-sharing system. Despite attempts to label Athens 'Parthenon Valley' and suggestions that the Sharing Economy sector is bringing €1.75billion to the tourist industry alone,[119] the Sharing Economy in Greece is a far cry from its Silicon Valley, venture capital backed counterpart, instead promoting the Greek values and heritage of the commons, democracy and community over profit.

ENTRANCE TO PALIOMYLOS ECO COMMUNITY AND ORGANIC FARM, EVIA, GREECE.

# THE TRAILBLAZER

**Mary Valiakas** is **35 years old** and is the **Greek founder of** *Oi Polloi*, a social enterprise that engages leading-edge thinkers, practitioners and big hearts into reimagining how society operates, using **Greece as a sandbox**.

" Sharing is a fundamental part of Greek culture, it's part of what it means to be human. Culturally, I grew up with hospitality as a central part of life. We were always welcoming people and hosting them. To be hospitable to strangers is a custom that goes all the way back to ancient times. There's a myth that some travellers visited an old couple who were very poor. They showed them hospitality by sharing food, shelter and everything they had with them – it turns out they were gods in disguise, so it's embedded in our culture to be hospitable to strangers.

We're developing a platform that enables the sharing of skills, knowledge and ultimately would make money obsolete. We'd have a decentralised, universal basic income, which will solve a lot of problems. We want to create a renaissance of humanity, which sounds really big and lofty, but it's actually based on the idea that if you have freedom from necessity, you are free to do the things that make you the best human you can be, the highest expression of yourself. This is what the liberal arts meant in ancient Greece. We're asking what are the skills needed to be free today? What are the liberal arts of the 21st century? We are inviting people to help us imagine what this would be, we want to create the freedom that will enable us to create the conditions necessary for the renaissance of humanity. "

MARY VALIAKAS, FOUNDER OF OI POLLOI, AT HER AUNT'S HOME IN LONDON.

# THE KNOWLEDGE SHARER

**Alexandros Pagidas is a 36-year-old philosopher from Greece. He runs a knowledge Sharing platform called *Patreon*, which promotes the idea of philosophy as an activity rather than a product. Alexandros dares people to be wise.**

"Traditionally philosophers weren't paid for their work. Socrates said he treats wisdom the same way he treats beauty: when you ask for money for something beautiful, it's like prostitution. When you sell wisdom, it's like prostituting the soul. This is why philosophical activity was in the spirit of love and sharing. Most creative people, once they've crafted something, share it. I believe that the motive behind sharing comes from creation. The ancient Greeks believed that it's not the creator but the user that defines the value of something. In politics, it's not the politicians who legislate, but those who live under the policies who can assess whether those policies are good. I wanted to apply this idea to publishing online. I started Patreon, a place where you can upload your works and share them with the world. If you believe what I've written is of value, then you can become a patron, so instead of a financial exchange, we share, people can donate and subscribe to you, without prostituting wisdom. It's only when people accept and promote these ideas that you can have a moral, cultural transformation, where sharing becomes the norm.

When the Sharing Economy blew up in the US, it was something new, but for Greeks, we've been doing this for centuries. It's not unusual for someone to leave flowers and food on the doorstep of someone who has just moved into a neighbourhood. Recently, a friend came home to find a sticky note on his front door that said, 'You left your door open, so I closed it for you' – he had no idea who it was.

In Greece, people share in times of recession because they want to demonstrate their generosity; that their sharing is not determined by material affluence. The Greek word *meraki* means doing something with soul, for love, to share. When you do something for love, the result is procreation, you have more then you had. Ultimately, love is sharing, that's what *meraki* means."

# SHARING WITH REFUGEES

**Sarah Griffith** is 58 years old and the founder of *Bridge2*, a charity she created after the tsunami in 2005, which provides emergency help. Based on Sharing principles and a motto of 'no bureaucracy, no middlemen, no faffing', *Bridge2* is crowdfunded and run by volunteers. The charity gives people a way to earn a living, feel empowered and builds communities. At the time of this interview, Sarah was based in Greece running a 270-person refugee camp in Veria, with refugees from Syria and Iraq.

" We enable and empower people to move forward. If they've lost everything, we help feed, clothe and build housing. We also help them make a living. In Sri Lanka we set up a bag workshop for women to sustain themselves. After the tsunami, I saw an image on CNN of a woman in a bus on its side swirling in tsunami waters, she was reaching for a helicopter but went under water. I saw her pained face and that was my light bulb moment, I decided to do something. Next I went to help in the aftermath of the Haitian earthquake, then to the Philippines following the typhoon and on to the Nepalese earthquake. In 2014, I saw what was happening with the refugee crisis, I got on the ferry to Calais to see for myself. I spent two days listening to horrendous stories. I've collected dead bodies, I've seen people shot, the tragedy of these stories left my conscious mind in limbo. I went home, put an appeal out. I ended up with a team of 21 people, builders, carpenters, architects and Sam, my son. We built a kitchen in Calais in two days. It fed 1,500 people a day for a year.

Do you know why I do what I do? I feel guilty about what our government is doing. I live in a first world country listening to people who have first world problems. (It puts things in perspective.) I don't want handbags, I don't want fancy shoes, I don't want to go to parties and drive nice cars, I just want to live.

I'm so lucky that I have my health and my boys and my house. More people need to realise that there shouldn't be borders in this world, we need to help each other. We are too worried about what people think of us, how they view our body image. We should all be helping someone else.

Sharing comes naturally, we have to share, it's the only way to make people realise we are all the same, we are brothers and sisters. We must share what we have. The work I do is epitomised by sharing. People are donating their money to me, I'm getting things for others to have and sharing with them. It's a two-way street and they share back with their humanity, humility, their stories and their appreciation. I will share the last thing I have if somebody's got less than me. "

TOP: KIDS PLAYING BACKGAMMON; BELOW LEFT: BANNER, REFUGEE CENTRE, CITY PLAZA HOTEL; BELOW RIGHT: SARAH GRIFFITHS, STATUE OF THE RESCUE OF HIPPODAMIA BY KING THESEUS, THE GREAT REFORMER, VICTORIA SQUARE, ATHENS, GREECE.

# SHARING: THE INDIAN WAY

By 2050, India will be home to 1.7 billion people, achieving the title of the world's most populated country, outsizing China in 2022.[120] This dynamic, socially entrepreneurial, emerging economy sees this as an opportunity to turn the necessary sharing of resources into a new socioeconomic system. With mobile usage set to become second to the US, and an average age of 26 (making up almost 50% of the population),[121] the Sharing Economy is increasingly being seen as the next best thing to happen to India.

From transport to hospitality, food, goods and jobs, sectors are being disrupted, reimagined and rebuilt as resource efficient, socially conscious systems and innovations are taking hold: Massively Open Online Courses (MOOCs), where users can access the learning they need when they need it; low-cost micro-enterprises launched via 'gig' platforms; co-living communities, like CoHo, offering housing options; and stress-free shared commuting services from Shuttl.

This significant shift, enabled by technology, is taking India back to its roots and has more in common with the philosophy of Gandhi than the consumerist tendencies of the past 20 years. The culture of sharing and philanthropy is as old as India itself, where someone who enjoys abundance without sharing is considered a thief according to the ancient Hindu scripture, the *Bhagavad Gita*. Indeed, 84% of the Indian population gives at least once a year.[122] No wonder, then, that the values of the Sharing Economy are appealing. India is also the first country worldwide to enshrine corporate giving into law. Since 2014, companies with annual revenues of over 10 billion rupees (£110 million) are required to give away 2% of their net profit to charity. And the law goes further, specifying that profits can be invested in education, poverty, gender equality and hunger.

Ownership, which had become a symbol of status within modern Indian society, is being challenged. Why waste precious resources owning, when you can make and save money accessing shared goods, enabling others less fortunate to benefit simultaneously? Though this is still far from the prevailing view, Sharing marketplaces are seeing considerable uptake from a millennial population who are embracing new lifestyles. A new, greener, caring, sharing India is emerging; while recycling is certainly not there yet, there are some encouraging signs that it will be.

MARINE DRIVE, MUMBAI, INDIA.

# A DAY IN THE LIFE OF A MUMBAI SHARER

**Bijal Doshi is passionate about sharing. This is a typical day in her life.**

### 06:00 to 07:00

**❝ It gives me immense joy to see someone else share and be instrumental in that, it comes from the deepest part of me. I support Rita to do this not for her, or the dogs, it's for me. Sharing is to help every human being, animal, or bird, grow from strength to strength. I feel there's an abundance, so it's important to share.**

### 10:00 to 15:00

The dream with the school is to educate women. It was set up by my grandfather and now we have educated 6,700 girls. I believe that there cannot be a conscientious society without educating women. I want to be instrumental in battling against the debilitating bias that exists.

### 16:00 to 17:00

Every day, I come here to give money to Chotelal Gupta, the Sev Puri Wala, so he can give sandwiches to the people that live in the hutment (slum) next to the building I live in. The money supports him, as well as the slum dwellers. In India, we like to make sure that everyone is fed. We never see food wasted, that's possibly why people here aren't dying of hunger. Western culture wastes so much more food. Here, people distribute surplus to the poor. From dawn until dusk,

**I take every opportunity to share, to light the light in someone who needs it. ❞**

DAY IN THE LIFE: 06.00 TO 07.00: BIJAL DOSHI (57) WITH SLUM DWELLER, RITA SHARING FOOD AT SUNRISE WITH STREET DOGS, PRIYADARSHINI PARK, MALABAR HILL; 10.00 TO 15.00: BIJAL DOSHI SHARING WITH STUDENTS AT P.N. DOSHI WOMEN'S COLLEGE, A SCHOOL FOR UNDERPRIVILEGED GIRLS; 16.00 TO 17.00: BIJAL DOSHI WITH CHOTELAL GUPTA GIVING A SLUM GIRL SEV PURI, ASHA NAGAR HUTMENT; BIJAL DOSHI, MARINE DRIVE, MUMBAI, INDIA.

# THE SOCIAL ENTREPRENEURS

Karen D'Souza (34) and Girish Agarwal (44) run *UnLtd India*, an organisation established in Mumbai in 2007, which finds, funds and supports early stage social entrepreneurs. Social entrepreneurs create shared value for society and the planet through their enterprises.

**Karen:** Over the past decade, India has given birth to some amazing social entrepreneurs, all of them are dreamers. They invite people into their dream with their energy and prove that it's possible to make an idea happen when you share it. They pull together the resources needed to make societal change and that makes them part of the Sharing Economy.

**Girish:** One characteristic I've noticed is the drive to achieve their purpose. Think about Mahatma Gandhi who started a movement with a purpose. What differentiates someone who succeeds as a social entrepreneur is how long they are willing to endure.

**Karen:** As Indians, I believe we have a unique brand of resilience because the odds are stacked against us. Resources are hard to come by, regulations are difficult. It is hard enough to get up and challenge the status quo, without having to deal with a lack of family support, which is a big problem for social entrepreneurs here, because families feel they should be the only priority, rather than wider issues. Despite this, the success rate of our organisations is high: our entrepreneurs have reached 2.5 million beneficiaries and have created 150,000 jobs. We are encouraging the sharing movement because we cannot create change on a large scale without sharing. We are building an ecosystem of change-makers that can leverage each other, multiplying the change we are making.

**Girish:** More young people are exploring social entrepreneurship. India will produce a significant number of social impact makers – people who are invited to be part of government, others who are invited by international organisations to speak about and share their projects so they can be replicated in other countries. 

TOP: SOCIAL ENTREPRENEURS AT UNLTD INDIA MEETUP, WORKBAY CO-WORKING, SANTA CRUZ, MUMBAI; UNLTD INDIA AWARDEES: INIR PINHEIRO, GRASSROUTES, DEHNA VILLAGE; AARTI NAIK, SAKHI SCHOOL FOR GIRLS EDUCATION, MULUND; ASHOK RATHOD, OSCAR FOUNDATION, MUMBAI.

> **"** There is a lot of power in sharing ideas, and today with technology, it does not take much for an idea to travel across the globe. Now, through sharing, social entrepreneurs have the ability to change the status quo across the world. **"**

**Karen D'Souza, UnLtd India who empower social entrepreneurs**

# THE CAT RESCUERS

In 2010, Mridu Khosla (34), Jason Moss (31) and Charu Khosla (31) set up an organisation to rescue injured and abandoned cats. Five years later, they established the *Cat Café Studio*, a sharing space for people and animals, where visitors can love, play with and adopt abandoned cats. To date they have rescued over 500 felines.

**Jason:** First we financed this through our creative agency. We used to keep the back window open at the office and started feeding cats. Before we knew it, there were lots and we were picking up injured kittens found on the streets. We moved to a bigger space, so we could serve coffee and tea to cat adopters and the Cat Café Studio was born. Within a year, we got so busy that we didn't have space on weekends.

**Charu:** I oversee the medical aspect of the rescues, my job is to get them from being sick, injured cats to healthy, adoptable cats. I love to see the transformation.

**Mridu:** The idea was to have a sustainable model, we had to find a way of generating revenue. All the money made from the café goes into cat care.

**Charu:** A big part of sharing is the love that people share with the cats, that's important for both humans and animals. The three of us care so much for these cats, they're our children and we are sharing them with a lot of strangers.

**Jason:** The sharing aspect is central to this space. You can connect with like-minded people who share your views.

**Mridu:** We wanted to build a shared space to show that humans and animals can co-exist. You can have a coffee with an animal in your lap. We see people using this as a co-working space, coming in with their colleagues, to write novels, even have a date here.

**Charu:** We are animal lovers and in this country, we were always outcasts. India needed a space to acknowledge us. This has become the first of its kind, where animal lovers can come, share and be proud. Attitudes towards animals are starting to change in India and we've been part of that change.

COOL CATS: (L TO R) JASON MOSS, MRIDU AND CHARU KHOSLA, CAT CAFÉ STUDIO; LAPPING IT UP: MANSI GHAG AND PRIYA JOSHI, CAT CAFÉ STUDIO, MUMBAI, INDIA.

# ENTREPRENEURS IN THE NEW ECONOMY

**Akshay Bhatia is 26 years old and lives in Mumbai. He is the founder of *Mutterfly*, a Sharing network that lets you rent and borrow items from people nearby. The name is inspired by butterflies, who only seek resources from their immediate surroundings.**

" The average Indian is not able to afford what they want, so Mutterfly is empowering people to live their lives without buying assets. We are bringing the concept of de-ownership, helping people to own less and experience more. It's the ability to change lives that drives me to do this, the joy of giving to someone who does not have that item, like the college student who rented a calculator for a two-hour exam.

The Sharing Economy is new to India, but there are cultural aspects that have to be addressed for a Sharing service to be adopted here. We are a service-based country, we have drivers and maids to take care of our daily needs. Bigger companies have had to adapt. Amazon delivers packages to people's houses and also picks up returns, which it does not do in other countries. We cannot function purely as platforms, we have to provide an end-to-end service. At first, people asked, 'How do we trust you?' We realised that we had to ensure safety, trust and deal with the logistics. We have 'delivery executives' who check the condition of the items, pick up, deliver them to the renter, and at the end of the rental, check and return them to the borrower.

India is a very ownership-centric country. If you own more, you have made it, ownership is a metric of success. People do not want to use something that is someone else's, from a status or hygiene perspective. We've had to educate people that what matters is the utility, not the ownership and show them that sharing makes economic sense. Our average customer saves £600 a year.

The growth potential for the Sharing Economy here is huge. If this becomes mainstream, it will change lives, because resources could be spent on nutrition, health and happy living. Most of our purchases are spent on consumer goods that don't enrich our lives.

The Sharing Economy is a great leveller; it's removing class differences. If I am a high-class lender, I am empowering the buyer. It's democratising experiences, people can access lifestyles for the day, and luxury is no longer the domain of the wealthy. Sharing is the foundation of the emerging economy because there are finite resources, the more we share, there are more chances for everyone to prosper. "

AKSHAY BHATIA, FINANCIAL DISTRICT, MUMBAI, INDIA; THE TIMES THEY ARE A-CHANGIN': GRAFFITI WALLS, MUMBAI, INDIA.

WE ARE EQUAL..
हम एक बराबर है।

REDUCE    REUSE    RECYCLE for a HAPPIER EARTH.

KEEP CALM!

KEEP CALM
YOU'LL FIND YOUR WAY.

# CONCLUSION

WHO LOOKS OUTSIDE DREAMS

TRUS

COME AS YOU ARE

FOOD, ART &

TRUST CAFE, AMSTERDAM

> **❝I feel most comfortable and most abundant when things are very simple and I know where everything is and there's nothing around that I don't need.❞**
>
> **Leonard Cohen, singer-songwriter, poet**

> **❝You cannot live without sharing, we share the air we breathe, whatever is alive is dependent on something else for its living. The plants wouldn't be able to live without the sun they depend on. We depend on sharing to be alive. I hope we become more aware of it and do it under the right conditions so that we can all flourish, I look forward to that future.❞**
>
> **Alexandros Pagidas, Greek philosopher, founder of Patreon**

Generation Share set out to bring the human stories of Sharing to life, to better understand the people behind the phenomenon known as the Sharing Economy – a system to live by where we care for people and planet and share available resources however we can. This book is the culmination of a decade-long expedition into the world of Sharing. Our journey to meet the people who are driving world change has been a study of age, gender, urban and rural living, wealth, culture, disability and geography in relation to the Sharing that makes us human. But it is also an exploration of the relationship between Sharing and the Sharing Economy, the final destination for this adventure.

Each story has offered a different insight into the life of a Sharer leading change in big and small ways. Each perspective demonstrates one of the five parts: categories, subsets, mode, values or impact of the Sharing Economy.

We've met Ashod Rathod who is sharing a love of football to educate and offer a future to slum kids in India; Saasha Celestial-One who through food-sharing app Olio believes we can end world hunger; there's intrapreneur Nanjira Sambuli transforming the lives of women across Africa by sharing access to digital technology; we've visited Georgia Haddad Nicolau who is spearheading citizen innovation in Latin America, and grandma Alia Dasouqi who has been empowered by hosting shared dinners in her home in Jaffa, Israel. We've been fascinated by Malik Yakitini at D-Town Farm in Detroit, USA, who is campaigning for food justice, and Australian Paralympic athlete Elizabeth Wright, who uses positivity and character building to inspire schoolkids. We can't forget the passion of Tamar Ben Shalom, who set up an urban kibbutz in the most impoverished, polluted neighbourhood in Jerusalem and embarked on a mission to bring the birds back, or the courage of Coen van de Steeg in the Netherlands, who, while recovering from a brain injury, created Sharing platform WeHelpen to connect communities to support each other. We've been inspired by pioneer Dr Natalie Shenker whose human milk bank is saving the lives of premature babies through donor milk sharing; we've been motivated by rebel innovators Ruth and Amy Anslow who are revolutionising the food industry through their supermarket HISBE, built on fair trade, customer collaboration and ethical sourcing. We've had a window into the worlds of mentor-sharer Anj Handa, who is transforming the lives of abused and disempowered women, and Palestinian farmer, teacher, footballer and role model Haitham Deeb, who is enabling peace by sharing love and motivation as an alternative to violence. We've been offered hope by the Sharers behind trust cafés, repair shops, share sheds, fab labs, eco-farms and open kitchens, demonstrating that the landscape of the existing Sharing Economy is vast and varied.

We've learned from Jacob Berkson how Sharing is so very visible when you are disabled, but that we are all reliant on it, we just 'invisibilise the sewage worker' and the people who make our clothes; we've discovered via Matan Israeli how sharing creates 'security for us all and takes away the need for insecurity'. Thanks to Natasha Wood, we've realised the power of sharing laughter to challenge stereotypes and help us to see one another as human beings, and Holly Tiffen has shown us how supporting community food growers can keep twice as much money in the local economy. Dr Olga Kesidou, who spearheaded a solidarity health clinic in Greece providing free medical care to refugees and those below the breadline, has opened our eyes to the impact of self-organised community action, and Shaff Prabatani, who works with excluded communities, has explained how inclusivity and sharing are two sides of the same coin. We've listened to the creator of Book Love, Samantha Williams, illuminate the importance of sharing cultural diversity and its impact on identity and self-worth, and we've been amazed by the bravery of Iman Bibars, who created the first micro-credit programme for women in the Arab world, giving them identities, a legal existence and financial freedom.

Through *Generation Share*, we've seen the impact of Sharing, from Alex Stephany's Beam platform, which crowdfunds training and employment for homeless people, to Aarti Naik with her Sakhi School for Girls Education, who contacted me from her slum in Mumbai to make sure that her story of sharing skills and a future with slum-based girls was included in this book.

*Generation Share* has taken us beyond the myths and the media headlines to reveal the diversity and the power of the Sharing Economy to change and save lives through the awe-inspiring stories of the change-makers who are living and creating it. It shows, unequivocally, the shift that is happening in the world; the tech-enabled, re-balancing of power and wealth that is taking place and that knows no boundaries of age, sex, culture, disability, class or geography. *Generation Share* see themselves as ordinary folk with a passion to create much-needed change. They are young, old, middle-aged; they come from all ethnic backgrounds and religions; they are disabled, able-bodied, men, women, non-binary, transgender, hyper gender; they live in densely populated cities and in villages; they are rich, poor and middle class; they live on every continent.

This is a pan-generational, pan-geographical, pan-economic, pan-gender group. They demonstrate explicitly that Sharing knows no boundaries. Generation Share, rather than a demographic, is a mindset, a lifestyle that we can choose to adopt. It represents a new consciousness that is emerging, an awareness that consumption doesn't lead to happiness or wellbeing, but that through Sharing, caring for people and planet and harnessing the power of technology for good, we can create a more equal, human, happy, healthy, resource efficient, connected and sustainable economy.

Sharing is everywhere, if we look for it. It's in our homes, our communities, our schools, our businesses, our cities, our villages. It's within each of us, in unlimited supply. Sharing isn't an age thing, a gender thing, a culture thing; it's simply a human thing. As *Generation Share* shows, to share is to be human.

**February 26th, 2018**

Dear Benita and Sophie,

A year ago, I wrote to you from my slum-based school for girls in Mumbai. I told you that I had heard about your project Generation Share and believed I should be part of it. Thank you for coming all the way from Brighton in England, to Mulund in Mumbai, India, and giving me the chance to share my story of the Sakhi School for Girls. I firmly believe that 'sharing' is the most powerful way to address and break the vicious cycle of poverty that many of us face. Through my sharing project, I have managed to create wealth which can bring positive changes in the lives of slum-based girls and women. By sharing my story in your book, I hope to ensure that every girl will able to continue her school education confidently with quality learning.

Thank you for your continued sharing, support and kind guidance to me,

Aarti Naik, Young Girl Change-maker

# THE PHOTOGRAPHER

Sophie Sheinwald **(49)** is an award-winning visual storyteller who specialises in photography with purpose. The camera is her excuse to make meaningful connections. She is the photographer and co-creator of *Generation Share*.

**"**Did I know what I was getting myself into when I said 'yes' to Benita? No. When she told me that she wanted to bring the visual element of sharing to life, I was struck by her positive drive and didn't hesitate to join her. But how could I capture the often intangible concept of sharing? Looking at the heart of this subject was fascinating. Ask a child to share and you'll often get resistance, suspicion and maybe tears. And with adults too, it can take some barriers to push through. So sharing strikes me as an ability. In meeting and photographing inspiring people who are unafraid to share, I felt I was at the heart of human connection.

One of the beautiful things I observed was when people talk about what they contribute to the world, their eyes light up. That's what I aimed to capture and share. So as Benita interviewed each person, I saw their sparkle and photographed them. We used this formula for most of the change-makers. I don't think many of them realised how much they had impacted on their communities until they shared their story with us.

Sharing involves trust and trust is what Benita and I often talked about. Trust that once you make a decision, all will fall into place. What seemed like a difficult task to achieve was my idea of how to photograph our Challenge Sharer, Sarah Burrell. She invites conversations with travellers on the London Underground to challenge biases about disability and inclusion. I wanted to capture her in action and for it to be authentic – not staged. While we were on the tube, Sarah started a conversation with a woman who was clearly engaged. Fortunately, she was also happy to be photographed and while they talked, I snapped away. This synchronicity seems to raise the vibration of the space. It opened the doors to a bit of magic. There have been several of these occurrences throughout this project.

As a visual storyteller I am sharing with you the world that I see. It's a bit like sharing a thought that's been created in 2D. I assess the scene, decide on a viewpoint, capture the moment and present it, so you can immerse yourself in the story and – hopefully – be inspired. **"**

SOPHIE SHEINWALD (L) AND BENITA MATOFSKA (R) AT THEIR WEEKLY FRIDAY MEETINGS FOR GENERATION SHARE, WORLD PEACE CAFE, BODHISATTVA BUDDHIST CENTRE, HOVE, UK.

# THE CHIEF SHARER AND AUTHOR

" My name is Benita Matofska, I'm 51 years old, a public speaker, global Sharing Economy expert and change-maker. This is what sharing means to me:

Sharing is smart, Sharing is kind,
An approach to life, a state of mind.
Sharing is knowing, Sharing is giving
Sharing is life, Sharing is living.
Sharing is doing, taking action
A fundamental interaction.
Sharing is meaning, Sharing is why
Sharing is something we need to try.
Sharing is vital, a proper noun
The heart of a community, village or town
Sharing is brave, how it should be
Sharing is shrewd, an inevitability.
Sharing is wonder, Sharing is family
Sharing is basic, Sharing is necessary
Sharing is truth, Sharing is vulnerability
Sharing is hope, Sharing is humanity.
Sharing is truth, it's learning to see
Sharing is infinite circularity
Sharing is our future and my vocation
Sharing is our only destination. "

# THANKS FOR SHARING!

*Generation Share* could never have been made without the love, support and Sharing we received at home and around the world from those who sustained, encouraged, fed, watered, housed and entertained us on our incredible journey. From couch-surfing to meal-sharing, we've created *Generation Share* through the Sharing Economy and by the very values that this book represents. Writing a book is never easy and as a lover of literature, I have absolute respect for anyone who has been brave and willing enough to endure the sleep deprivation needed to pen their ideas. I couldn't have done this without the support of my gorgeous family: my husband and soulmate Lee Dyer, who not only held the fort while I was on my many travels, handled teenage woes, covered my share of the household chores, but also cleverly created the *Generation Share* style frames, cover concept and infographic; my beautiful daughter and wonder teen-chef Maia Matofska-Dyer for supplying delicious snacks, teas (occasional meals) and words of inspiration to keep me going when I was at the end of my rope; astute son Sol for ideas, witticisms and left-field questions that got me thinking and writing, plus the odd break playing kitchen football; Buster the dog for cuddles and being my walking companion (in his own time) when I needed air. None of this would have happened without the support of my loving parents Linda and Alan Harris (Nini and Popski), who taught me the values and importance of Sharing from an early age. Even at my lowest moment, they never lost their faith in me that I would find a way to get this book published and for my dad's never-ending positivity (he's the source), enthusiasm and recycled jokes that put a smile on my face on our daily, early morning calls. I can't forget to mention my dearest friend Joey Silverman in California who was the first person to literally kick-start our Kickstarter campaign and help get this project on the road. Thanks to Clare Kandola, my partner at The People Who Share, for words of wisdom and many a glass of Prosecco; Sarah Tohill and the Dulcetones choir for recharging my soul and letting me sing my heart out when needed, and my rock of a buddy Julie Kaye, for always being at the end of the phone to listen to my woes, offer wisdom and make me laugh; Davel Patel for

being the whirlwind that arrives from her current overseas posting changing the world, and makes me giggle with her ferocious passion, intensity and oblivion for the calendar; Jo (Nimrita) Kaur and her extraordinary Kundalini yoga classes that helped me flow and kept me strong; Kate Hackworth for wise insights and being a sounding board; super volunteer Vidit Jain in Mumbai, who painstakingly transcribed over a hundred interviews and without whom there would not be a book! Elodie Lod, Josie Beasley, Liz Sleeper and Heather Johns for additional transcription and Ileen Kohn in New York for Spanish translation. But my biggest thanks go to dear friend Sophie Sheinwald, for being crazy enough to accept my invite to join me on this unbelievable escapade to co-create *Generation Share*. It's true to say she had no idea what she was letting herself in for (which is fortunate). It's been extraordinary, challenging, mind-boggling, hilarious, inspiring, bloody hard graft, but most of all magic. Our friendship goes deep (we definitely tested it at times) and now goes deeper. We've shared (almost) everything (notably the smallest bed ever, at an Airbnb in Barcelona, and a composting loo, in the dark at Paliomylos in Greece). *Generation Share* has taken us on an unforgettable voyage to the core of what it means to be human. A big thanks too, to Sophie's family, Ashley, Ayana and Jada Sheinwald, for their love, patience and most of all for sharing (or rather letting me commandeer) so much of Sophie's time to make *Generation Share* a reality. I know Sophie couldn't have co-created this book with me if it weren't for the wonderful mums and dads who helped with childcare while we were travelling, so a big thank you to Lisa Mighall, Eri and Dan Skinner, Liz Gogerly and Tara Hammerstad.

Thanks to my public speaking agent, Michael Levey at Speaking Office, for ongoing support and for suggesting I find a good literary agent to secure the right publisher. That literary agent turned out to be the wise Jaime Marshall who kindly introduced us to the wonderful Ali Shaw and the brilliant team at Bristol University and Policy Press who were brave enough to take this project on. Special thanks to editor Rebecca Tomlinson and the wonderful

Kathryn King in marketing for always being willing to go the extra mile, and Tim Mahar on sales. But most of all to the incredible (and patient) production editor Ruth Wallace who has endured my daily calls, questions and emails and has been willing to find a way to make the most sustainable book we could. Sorry you won't be around for launch as you'll be sharing your time with your new baby and here's to the magical journey that is motherhood. Thanks for believing in *Generation Share* and helping to make it happen, despite our agent provocateurism! A huge thanks and hats off to Chris Wilson and the design team at blu inc. in Bristol who had not only two strong-willed, design opinionated women to deal with, but our husbands too, since we are both married to designers – me to Emmy award-winning motion graphic designer and artist, Lee Dyer, and Sophie to service design aficionado, Ashley Sheinwald. Thanks to Lee and Ashley for their valuable contributions, it was for sure, a collaborative process. Chris, I know it wasn't easy and I have absolute admiration for the work that blu inc. put in to deliver such a distinct book that we are so very proud of.

For hosting us and making us welcome: Filipa Belo and Catia Curica from Organi on the trip to Portugal where our adventure began, Georgia and the team at The Dorm in the LX Factory on that same trip, Candida Rato for leaving her mountain retreat to be our Lisbon guide for the weekend, Galit Shvo, Yair Freedman, Eyal Bloch, Zafrir Bloch-David from WEconomize in Israel, who made our incredible trip to Share Israel possible, and for sharing delicious Israeli food, knowledge, insights and introducing us to change-makers, Firas Hamad and the students of the Ahmad Sameh Peace School in East Jerusalem and Khaled Abu Khalaf and the Palestinian women leaders from the Sur Baher Community Centre in East Jerusalem; Mary Valiakas and Oi Polloi in Greece, for finding stories, driving and joining us on our unforgettable and hilarious Evia adventure, Mary's lovely parents George and Geraldine Valiakas in Athens for putting us up, Marcus Letts from Transform Evia for connecting us with so many change-makers in Greece, Giorgos Vallis and the community at Paliomylos for delicious handmade vegan, gluten free pizza and a special stay, Samantha van den Bos in Amsterdam for sharing her gorgeous apartment and being super generous, ShareNL for sharing transport and drinks by the canal, Nanette Schippers from the City of Amsterdam for connecting us with a network of Sharers in the city, Chiara, Silvino and the team at WithLocals, Gina Farish in Barcelona for making our incredible Spanish trip happen, the wonderful super connector, Albert Cañigueral, Aviva Adda for her personalised Barcelona tour, and Dog Buddy Barcelona. Thanks also to Inés Echevarria from sustainable fashion brand Uttopy and crowdfunding blog CrowdHub.es for sharing insights; the Ouishare Fest team in Paris for all their support, Bijal Doshi in Mumbai, who was the hostess with the mostess and made our India trip so special, UnLtd India for connecting us with incredible change-makers and hosting a *Generation Share* Meet Up, sisters Michelle, Rochelle and family in Mumbai for scrumptious lunches; Phyllis Santamaria for a gorgeous lunch in her London flat, the staff and pupils from Brodetsky Primary School in Leeds (coincidentally my primary school!) who welcomed us into their classrooms to photograph Elizabeth Wright and share memories. A particular thanks to David Murphy and the Human Flourishing Project in Nottingham for sharing time and incredible insights into the world of human flourishing. Thanks to Will Waghorn for lending us his microphone to record vlogs in Lisbon and Israel. We can't forget the many random acts of kindness from the man who helped us on the train with our camera equipment at Ourq train station in Paris, the entrepreneurs who shared their plug on the train home from Totnes so Sophie could download and edit photos and so many others whose warmth and care carried us on our journey. Thanks to the Brighton Buddhist Centre café where Sophie and I spent over 500 hours working on this project, with our weekly Friday meetings and 'emergency sessions' who welcomed us even when they were closed with hot cups of tea and vegan chocolate! Thanks too, to all those Sharers who we interviewed for this book but who sadly didn't make the final version, your insights and sharing has helped make this possible.

We are so grateful to all 129 incredible Sharers (below), friends, family, colleagues and others who kindly supported our crowdfunding campaign on Kickstarter, which paid for our travel and got *Generation Share* on the road. You are:

Agnyte Mil, Aladin Aladin, Alan Harris, Allen Greenwood, Ami Shpiro, Andy Peck, Angela Samuels, Anna Beattie, Anne Ravanona, Arie Ben David, Avril Harris, Barbara Fagan Sullivan, Billee Howard, Brian Downey, Carroll Lloyd, Catey Sexton, Charlotte Rustin, Claire Robilliard, Clare Kandola, Claudia Cuseta, Davel Patel, David Goodman, David King, Deb Freeman, Debbie Ross, Donnie Maclurcan, Elissa Bayer, Eoghan Parle, Erika Whiting, Erin, Eva Edel, Eve Laird, Evelyn Day, Florent Thurin, Francis Sealey, Fraser Laing, Gabriella Polletta, Gary Coyle, Gene Homicki, Gina Farish, Graeme Risby, Greg Whitfield, Hazel and Gil Victor, Hilary Ellis, Humphrey Bowles, James Alexander, Jan Rickers, Jane Greening, Jane Robbie, Janet Kay, Janine Levy, Jen Gale, Jennifer Stevens, Jo Godden, Joe Silverman, John Grant, Johnny Webb, Joshua Tjon Herron, Jude Archery, Julia Bayer, Julie Kaye, Kasia Wilton, Kate Jackson, Kemi Ayoola, Kristin Wolff, Laure Claire Reillier, Lee Dyer, Linda Turner, Liz Watson, Louisa Goott, Louise Moshe, Louise Sigfrid, Lynne Davies, Madeleine Bridgett, Maria Ana, Mark Walker, Marshall Frieze, Mary Valiakas, Matt Desmier, Michael Daniel, Michelle Cundle, Moni Pineda and Mike Vargas, Moyra Scott, Naomi Okin, Neal Gorenflo and the team from Shareable, Nick Bright, Nick Holden, Nicki Alvey Bazlinton, Nicky Chisolm, Nicola Bahar, Nicolas Mouart, Nicole Dewindt, Nina Emett, Olivia Sibony, Patrick Aylmer, Paul Sternberg, Phyllis Santamaria, Pins Brown, Robert Eden, Roberta Papini, Ron Bahar, Ruth Anslow, Ruth Gottlieb, Ruth Sadik, Sarah Bennet, Sarah McLoughlin, Shaffique Prabatani, Sharon Starr, Silvia Arnone, Sophie Key, Stephanie Crechriou, Stephen Cheifitz, Sue Bradley, Tanya Wynne, Tessa Cook, Tessy Britton, Tiffany Leeson, Tim Buick, Tim Clark, Timo Peach, Uli Kindermann, Veronica Poku, Victoria Orlianges, Wendy Shaw, William Shaw, Yael Breuer, Yair Friedman and the team from WEconomize.

A few crowdfunders secured a special mention and here are their thoughts on what sharing means to them:

**Sharing to me means sharing time with people to overcome their age loneliness by entertaining them with my ukulele! It's about sharing happy times, love and sharing mutual satisfaction.**

Alan Harris

**When my heart beats in harmony with the world's heart, the joy of sharing becomes the natural thing to do.**

Arie Ben David

**Sharing means enriching people's lives. And the most wonderful thought is that everyone has an inner sharer just waiting to be unlocked.**

Humphrey Bowles, Guardhog, Sharing Economy insurance

**To share is to let people into your heart and to give, it enriches your very soul.**

Ruth Sadik

1 Mark Dyble et al (2016) Networks of Food Sharing Reveal the Functional Significance of Multilevel Sociality in Two Hunter-Gatherer Groups, *Current Biology*, 26(15): 2017–21.

2 An American TV sitcom, starring Henry Winkler as The Fonz, that presented an idealised vision of life in the 1950s.

3 Annie Leonard (2010) *The Story of Stuff*, Simon and Schuster.

4 Share The World's Resources (2012) Financing the Global Sharing Economy, Report published by Share The World's Resources: www.sharing.org/information-centre/reports/financing-global-sharing-economy

5 A term coined by mathematician and pioneer of chaos theory Edward Lorenz, showing how small changes can lead to larger differences.

6 All interview content including statistics, facts, references, company names and occupations were correct at the time of recording. All ages correspond to the age of the interviewee at the time the photograph was taken (between October 2016 and November 2018).

7 American Planning Association (2014) Investing in Place: Two Generations' view on the future of communities, p28: https://planning-org-uploaded-media.s3.amazonaws.com/legacy_resources/policy/polls/investing/pdf/pollinvestingreport.pdf

8 Sharing is the New Buying, Vision Critical and Crowd Companies, 2014: http://info.mkto.visioncritical.com/rs/visioncritical/images/sharing-new-buying-collaborative-economy.pdf

9 Is Sharing the New Buying? Nielsen, May 2014: www.nielsen.com/ke/en/insights/reports/2014/is-sharing-the-new-buying.html

10 The Sharing Economy: How Will it Disrupt Your Business? Megatrends: the collisions, PwC, August 2015: www.pwc.co.uk/blogs/migrated/sharing-economy-final_0814.pdf

11 Fiverr, August 2015: www.fiverr.com/news/seniors-gear-up-for-sharing

12 Neil Howe and William Strauss (1991) *Generations: The History of America's Future, 1584 to 2069*, William Morrow and Company, Inc.

13 Millennials Fuelling the Experience Economy, Eventbrite, Harris Interactive Poll and Report, June 2014, published online by Eventbrite: https://eventbrite-s3.s3.amazonaws.com/marketing/Millennials_Research/Gen_PR_Final.pdf. James Wallman (2015) *Stuffocation: Living More With Less*, Penguin.

14 Fast Company, March 2015: www.fastcompany.com/3027876/millennials-dont-care-about-owning-cars-and-car-makers-cant-figure-out-why. Millennials: Changing Consumer Behaviour, Goldman Sachs, Millennials, May 2015: www.goldmansachs.com/insights/archive/millennials/index.html

15 Social Value in the Collaborative Economy, Nesta and TNS Global Survey, November 2016: www.nesta.org.uk/news/younger-generation-adopting-sharing-economy-platforms-for-social-benefit-not-just-profit/

16 Maru/Matchbox, The Battle for Trust in the Sharing Economy Report, 2017: https://marumatchbox.com/resources/battle-trust-sharing-economy/

17 Jared Meyer, Manhattan Institute, author of *Uber-Positive: Why Americans Love the Sharing Economy*.

18 Maru/Matchbox, *The Battle for Trust in the Sharing Economy Report*.

19 PwC, Consumer Intelligence Series, The Sharing Economy, April 2015: www.pwc.com/us/en/industry/entertainment-media/publications/consumer-intelligence-series/assets/pwc-cis-sharing-economy.pdf

20 The term 'Generation X' was first coined by photographer Robert Capa in 1953 for a photo essay in *Picture Post* about the young people reaching adulthood immediately after the Second World War.

21 State of the Startup Report, Sage, 2015: www.sage.com/na/~/media/site/sagena/responsive/docs/startup/report

22 Millennial Branding and Monster, Multi-generational Entrepreneurship Attitudes Study, February 2013: http://millennialbranding.com/case-studies/monster-study/

23 PwC, Consumer Intelligence Series, The Sharing Economy, April 2015: www.pwc.com/us/en/industry/entertainment-media/publications/consumer-intelligence-series/assets/pwc-cis-sharing-economy.pdf

24 EY, Global Generations: A Global Study on Work-life Challenges Across Generations, 2015: www.ey.com/Publication/vwLUAssets/EY-global-generations-a-global-study-on-work-life-challenges-across-generations/$FILE/EY-global-generations-a-global-study-on-work-life-challenges-across-generations.pdf

25 The term 'Sandwich Generation' was introduced to the social work and the gerontology communities, respectively, by Dorothy Miller and Elaine Brody in 1981.

26 John Hughes' 1985 film *The Breakfast Club* became a Gen X cult classic along with Richard Linklater's 1990 film *Slacker*.

27 Jay Pritchett is the lead character in ABC's American hit TV mockumentary series *Modern Family*.

28 Gen Z Report: Get ready for the most self-conscious, demanding consumer segment, Fung Global Retail and Technology, August 2016: www.fbicgroup.com/sites/default/files/Gen%20Z%20Report%202016%20by%20Fung%20Global%20Retail%20Tech%20August%2029,%202016.pdf

29 Accounting Principles, Generation Z Vs Millennials, September 2017: www.accountingprincipals.com/employers/employer-resources/what-you-need-know-generation-z/

30 David Stillman and Jonah Stillman (2017) *Gen Z @ Work: How the Next Generation is Transforming the Workplace*, Harper Business.

31 The Common Sense Census: Plugged-In Parents of Teens and Tweens, Common Sense Media, 2016: www.commonsensemedia.org/research/the-common-sense-census-plugged-in-parents-of-tweens-and-teens-2016

32 JWT, Gen Z: Savvy, connected, want to change the world Report, May 2015: www.jwtintelligence.com/trend-reports/generation-z/. Creative Artist Agency/Intern Sushi, 2014: http://time.com/6693/coming-soon-to-your-office-gen-z/. 21st Century Learners: www.wlwv.k12.or.us/cms/lib/OR01001812/Centricity/Domain/1994/21st%20Century%20Learners.pdf

33 JWT, Gen Z: Savvy, connected, want to change the world Report, May 2015: www.jwtintelligence.com/trend-reports/generation-z/

34 US Department of Labour, Volunteering in the United States, 2015: www.bls.gov/news.release/volun.nr0.htm

35 Generation Nation: Redefining America's Boomers, Gen X, Millennials & Gen Z, 747 Insights, Collaborata, 2017: www.youtube.com/watch?v=gv0vww25b8Q; www.collaborata.com/blog/generation-nation-redefining-americas-boomers-xers-millennials-and-gen-z

36 David Stillman and Jonah Stillman (2017) *Gen Z @ Work: How the Next Generation is Transforming the Workplace*, Harper Business.

37 Generation Z: A Look at the Technology and Media Habits of Today's Teens, Gen Z: The Limitless Generation, Wikia, 2013.

38 David Stillman and Jonah Stillman (2017) *Gen Z @ Work: How the Next Generation is Transforming the Workplace*, Harper Business.

39 Historian and author Landon Jones (1980) *Great Expectations: America and the Baby Boom Generation*, Booksurge Publishing.

40 The term 'baby boomer' first appeared in a 1970 *Washington Post* article.

41 Harold Macmillan's 1957 speech in Bedford, UK, 'Let us be frank about it: most of our people have never had it so good.'

42 'Turn on, tune in, drop out' was a phrase made popular by Timothy Leary at the 1967 'Human Be-In' gathering at the Golden Gate Bridge in San Francisco.

43 Benita Matofska, The People Who Share, Global Sharing Week Survey, 2013 and What We Know About the Global Sharing Economy Report, 2014.

44 The On-Demand Economy Survey, Burson-Marsteller, January 2016: www.slideshare.net/Burson-Marsteller/the-ondemand-economy-survey

45 JP Morgan Chase, The Online Platform Economy: Has Growth Peaked? 2016: www.jpmorganchase.com/corporate/institute/document/jpmc-institute-online-platform-econ-brief.pdf

46 PwC, Consumer Intelligence Series, The Sharing Economy, April 2015: www.pwc.com/us/en/industry/entertainment-media/publications/consumer-intelligence-series/assets/pwc-cis-sharing-economy.pdf

47 Fractl, Average Facebook User Sharing Habits Study, April 2016: www.frac.tl/work/marketing-research/facebook-user-sharing-habits-study/

48 PetCloud, Baby Boomers dominate pet sharing economy, October 2017: www.medianet.com.au/releases/144905/

49 Home Sharing: A Powerful Option to Help Older Americans Stay in their Homes, Airbnb, November 2016: www.aarp.org/content/dam/aarp/livable-communities/documents-2016/Airbnb-HomeSharing-OlderAmericans-Report-11-2016.pdf

50 GirlsNotBrides.org: www.girlsnotbrides.org/about-child-marriage/

51 UN Women: www.unwomen.org/en/what-we-do/ending-violence-against-women/facts-and-figures

52 Tarana Burke is an American civil rights activist, known for being the first to use the phrase 'Me Too' in 2006, which later went on to become a two-word hashtag used on social media to help demonstrate the widespread prevalence of sexual assault and harassment, especially in the workplace.

53 Time's Up is a campaign launched on 1 January 2018 by 300 female Hollywood actors, agents, writers, directors and executives, to counter systemic sexual harassment in the entertainment business and workplaces.

54 Benita Matofska, TEDx Frankfurt, 'The Secret of the Sharing Economy', 2017. www.youtube.com/watch?v=-uv3JwpHjrw

55 Diane Coyle, The Sharing Economy in the UK Productivity Report, Sharing Economy UK, January 2016: www.sharingeconomyuk.com/perch/resources/210116thesharingeconomyintheuktpdc.docx1111.docx-2.pdf

56 Women Unbound: Unleashing female entrepreneurial potential, PwC and The Crowdfunding Centre, July 2017: www.pwc.com/womenunbound

57 Women Unbound: Unleashing female entrepreneurial potential, PwC and The Crowdfunding Centre, July 2017: www.pwc.com/womenunbound

58 Roberta Bampton and Patrick Maclagan (2009) Does a Care Orientation explain gender differences in ethical decision making? *Business Ethics: A European Review*, 18(2): https://doi.org/10.1111/j.1467-8608.2009.01556.x

59 Social Enterprise UK, The State of Social Enterprise Survey 2015: Leading the world in social enterprise, 2015, www.socialenterprise.org.uk/state-of-social-enterprise-report-2015

60 See www.nber.org/papers/w19277; https://hbr.org/2018/07/in-collaborative-work-cultures-women-carry-more-of-the-weight; https://greatergood.berkeley.edu/article/item/are_women_more_ethical_than_men; http://resource.owen.vanderbilt.edu/facultyadmin/data/research/2455full.pdf; http://psycnet.apa.org/doiLanding?doi=10.1037%2F0021-9010.82.6; www.telegraph.co.uk/women/womens-business/9957262/Women-make-better-bosses-than-men.html; www.inderscience.com/offer.php?id=52743; https://appointments.thetimes.co.uk/article/times-top-50-employers-for-women/; www.pwc.com/en/corporate-governance/publications/assets/pwc-acds-2014-the-gender-edition.pdf

61 Elliot Martin, Susan Shaheen, Impacts of Car2Go on Vehicle Ownership, Modal Shift, Vehicle Miles Traveled and Greenhouse Gas Emissions, UC Berkeley's Transportation Sustainability Research Center, July 2016: http://innovativemobility.org/wp-content/uploads/2016/07/Impactsofcar2go_FiveCities_2016.pdf

62 Food and Agriculture Organisation of the United Nations, 2016: www.fao.org/save-food/resources/keyfindings/en/

63 Julian Abel, Compassionate Frome Project, Compassionate Community Project, *Resurgence and Ecologist*, February 2018: www.resurgence.org/magazine/article5039-compassionate-community-project.html. Compassionate Frome Project: www.compassionate-communitiesuk.co.uk/projects/

64 Flash Eurobarometer 438 Report, The Use of Collaborative Platforms. Survey requested by the European Commission, Flash Eurobarometer 438, TNS Political & Social, June 2016.

65 Aaron Smith, Shared, Collaborative and On-Demand: The New Digital Economy Report, Pew Research Centre, May 2016: www.pewinternet.org/2016/05/19/the-new-digital-economy/

66 Sharing Cities: Activating the Urban Commons, published by Shareable, 2018 www.shareable.net/sharing-cities

67 Digital Economy Compass 2018, Statista: www.weforum.org/agenda/2018/03/internet-minute-whatsapp-facebook-emails/; www.statista.com/page/compass

68 Carl Benedikt Frey and Michael Osbourne, The Future of Employment, Oxford Martin School, Oxford University, 2013: www.oxfordmartin.ox.ac.uk/downloads/academic/future-of-employment.pdf. From Brawn to Brains: The impact of technology on jobs in the UK, Deloitte: www2.deloitte.com/content/dam/Deloitte/uk/Documents/Growth/deloitte-uk-insights-from-brawns-to-brain.pdf. The State of the State Report, Oxford University and Deloitte, 2016: www2.deloitte.com/content/campaigns/uk/the-state-of-the-state/the-state-of-the-state/the-state-of-the-state.html

69 Office of National Statistics, 2014: www.statistics.gov.uk/downloads/theme_compendia/RegionalSnapshot/rt43-rural-urban-areas.xls. See also: www.telegraph.co.uk/news/politics/11318308/Countryside-population-to-increase-dramatically-by-2025.html

70 John F. Helliwell, Hugh Shiplett, Christopher P. Barrington-Leigh, How happy are your neighbours? The National Bureau of Economic Research, May 2018: www.nber.org/papers/w24592. Dr Edel Walsh, University College Cork, European Social Survey, 2016: www.europeansocialsurvey.org/

71 Richard Percy, Countryside Living Index Quarterly Survey by NFU Mutual, Attitudes Towards Rural and Urban Life, 2012 and Office of National Statistics, 2014: www.statistics.gov.uk/downloads/theme_compendia/RegionalSnapshot/rt43-rural-urban-areas.xls

72 Listening to Sharing Economy Initiatives, Collaborating Centre on Sustainable Consumption and Production, Columbia Business School, Akatu Institute for Conscious Consumption, Shareable, Ouishare, 2015: www.scp-centre.org/wp-content/uploads/2016/05/Listening_to_Sharing_Economy_Initiatives.pdf

73 Marshall McLuhan coined the idea of a 'global village' in his books *The Gutenberg Galaxy: The Making of Typographic Man* (1962) and *Understanding Media* (1964), where he describes how the world has been contracted into a village by technology.

74 Transition Network: https://transitionnetwork.org/wp-content/uploads/2016/09/The-Essential-Guide-to-Doing-Transition.pdf page 5.

75 Jeremy Rifkin (2014) *The Zero Marginal Cost Society*, New York: St Martin's Press.

76 'Blockchain is an algorithm and distributed data structure for managing electronic cash without a central administrator among people who know nothing about one another.' Definition by Steve Wilson, Constellation Research: www.zdnet.com/article/blockchain-explained-in-plain-english/

77 Jeremy Rifkin, *The Zero Marginal Cost Society*.

78 Arun Sundararajan and Samuel P. Fraiberger, Peer-to-Peer Rental Markets in the Sharing Economy NYU Stern School of Business, 2017: https://papers.ssrn.com/sol3/papers.cfm?abstract_id=2574337

79 J. David-Pluess and R. Meiers, Business Leadership for an Inclusive Economy, A Framework for Collaboration and Impact, BSR, May 2015: www.bsr.org/reports/BSR_Inclusive_Economy_Paper_2015.pdf

80 Aaron Smith, Shared, Collaborative and On-Demand: The New Digital Economy Report, Pew Research Centre, May 2016: www.pewinternet.org/2016/05/19/the-new-digital-economy/

81 FareShare, 2018: https://fareshare.org.uk/what-we-do/our-impact/

82 Tribe Called Quest, 'Can I Kick It?', released 1990.

83 Iro Evlampidou and Manolis Kogevinas, Solidarity Outpatient Clinics in Greece: A Survey of a Massive Social Movement, Science Direct, 2018: www.sciencedirect.com/science/article/pii/S021391111830013X

84 Aaron Smith, Shared, Collaborative and On-Demand: The New Digital Economy Report, Pew Research Centre, May 2016: www.pewinternet.org/2016/05/19/the-new-digital-economy/

85 Fundly, 2017: https://blog.fundly.com/crowdfunding-statistics/. Forbes, CFX 2016: https://cfxtrading.com/research/10-equity-crowdfunding-statistics-that-should-have-your-attention-infographic

86 Daiva Kvedarate, Tapping the Potential of Social Enterprises, 2015: www.eesc.europa.eu/en/documents/tapping-potential-social-enterprises

87 Social Enterprise UK, The State of Social Enterprise Survey 2015: Leading the world in social enterprise.

88 Thanks to icebreaker for additional financial support, enabling The Transparent Sharer story to be included in *Generation Share*. Despite the challenges of distance and time zone, we are thrilled to be able to bring this important story to *Generation Share* readers.

89 Norhayati Zakaria and Leena Ajit Kaushal, *Global Entrepreneurship and New Venture Creation in the Sharing Economy*, Hershey, PA: IGI Global, 2017.

90 Clifford Geertz (1973) *The Interpretation of Cultures*, Basic Books.

91 Cristina Da Milano, The Shift, The Networked Economy, The Cultural Sector and Beyond Culture Action Europe (CAE), 2015 and 2017: https://cultureactioneurope.org/files/2017/02/CAE_SE_ToolkitY3_v3LP.pdf

92 Cristina Da Milano, The Shift, The Networked Economy, The Cultural Sector and Beyond Culture Action Europe (CAE), 2015 and 2017: https://cultureactioneurope.org/files/2017/02/CAE_SE_ToolkitY3_v3LP.pdf

93 Edgar Morin (2008) *On Complexity*, Hampton Press Inc.

94 The Atmel Corporation, 2015: www.extension.org/2015/11/03/ten-statistics-that-reveal-the-size-and-scope-of-the-maker-movement/

95 Matthew Crawford (2009) *Shop Class as Soulcraft*, Penguin.

96 Survey of Income and Program Participation, Americans with Disabilities Census, 1994-1995. Invisible Disabilities Association: https://invisibledisabilities.org/what-is-an-invisible-disability/

97 Is Britain Fairer? The state of equality and human rights, 2018, Equality and Human Rights Commission. www.equalityhumanrights.com/en/publication-download/britain-fairer-2018

98 An Inclusive Sharing Economy Report, Business Leaders for an Inclusive Economy, September, BSR 2016: www.bsr.org/reports/BSR_An_Inclusive_Sharing_Economy.pdf

99 S. Kathi Brown, The Sharing Economy, Challenges for People with Disabilities, AARP, December 2016: www.aarp.org/content/dam/aarp/research/surveys_statistics/econ/2016/sharing-economy-disabilities.doi.10.26419%252Fres.00141.001.pdf

100 Mason Amery, Sean Rogers, Lisa Schur, Douglas Kruse, No Room at the Inn, Disability Access in the New Sharing Economy, Rutgers University, May 2017: www.4wheeledlefty.com/wp-content/uploads/2017/06/disability_access_in_sharing_economy.pdf

101 Expat Insider: The World Through Expat Eyes, InterNations, 2017: https://cms-internationsgmbh.netdna-ssl.com/cdn/file/2017-09/Expat_Insider_2017_The_InterNations_Survey.pdf

102 John Helliwell, Richard Layard and Jeffrey Sachs (eds), *World Happiness Report*, New York: Sustainable Development Solutions Network, 2017, http://worldhappiness.report/ed/2017/

103 David McCandless, Information Is Beautiful, 2016: https://informationisbeautiful.net/visualizations/because-every-country-is-the-best-at-something/

104 World Economic Forum (WEF), Global Gender Gap Report, 2017: www.weforum.org/reports/the-global-gender-gap-report-2017

105 UN Human Development Report, 2017: http://hdr.undp.org/

106 David McCandless, Information Is Beautiful, 2016: https://informationisbeautiful.net/visualizations/because-every-country-is-the-best-at-something/

107 Nielsen, Is Sharing the New Buying? May 2014: www.nielsen.com/content/dam/corporate/us/en/reports-downloads/2014%20Reports/global-share-community-report-may-2014.pdf

108 Robert Vaughn, Assessing the size and value of the Collaborative Economy in Europe, PwC, European Commission, 2017: https://preview.thenewsmarket.com/Previews/PWC/DocumentAssets/440449.pdf

109 Kathleen Stokes, Emma Clarence, Lauren Anderson, April Rinne, Making Sense of the UK Collaborative Economy, Nesta, September 2014: https://collaborativeeconomy.com/wp/wp-content/uploads/2015/04/making_sense_of_the_uk_collaborative_economy_14.pdf; The State of the Sharing Economy, 2013, The People Who Share and Opinium: www.thepeoplewhoshare.com/tpws/assets/File/TheStateoftheSharingEconomy_May2013_FoodSharingintheUK.pdf

110 Rachel Griffiths, Cooperatives UK, The Great Sharing Economy, A report into sharing across the UK, 2013: http://library.uniteddiversity.coop/Cooperatives/The_great_sharing_economy.pdf

111 The State of the Sharing Economy, 2013, The People Who Share and Opinium: www.thepeoplewhoshare.com/tpws/assets/File/TheStateoftheSharingEconomy_May2013_FoodSharingintheUK.pdf

112 Andrew Bibby, 'The history of the British co-operative movement – timeline', *Guardian*, 29 January 2014: www.theguardian.com/social-enterprise-network/gallery/2014/jan/29/the-history-of-the-british-co-operative-movement-timeline

113 The Slang Dictionary, 1864, refers to military officers having a 'whip', with each man contributing a shilling for extra wine.

114 Wikipedia, Nov 2018: https://en.wikipedia.org/wiki/Nelson%27s_Column Guinness Book of Records 2015.

115 Diane Coyle and Sharing Economy UK, *The Sharing Economy in the UK*, 2016: www.sharingeconomyuk.com/publications

116 Robert Vaughn, Assessing the size and value of the Collaborative Economy in Europe, PwC, European Commission, 2017.

117 Global Sharing Week Survey, Survey Monkey, The People Who Share, 2017.

118 FareShare, 2018: https://fareshare.org.uk/what-we-do/our-impact/

119 The tax-paying ability of hotels and potential use of the sharing economy for the tax normalisation of the industry, Grant Thornton, Hellenic Hotels, 2017.

120 World Population Prospects, 2017, UN: https://population.un.org/wpp/

121 The Rise of the Sharing Economy: The Indian Landscape, EY, Nascom, Product Enclave, 2015: www.ey.com/Publication/vwLUAssets/ey-the-rise-of-the-sharing-economy/$FILE/ey-the-rise-of-the-sharing-economy.pdf

122 India Giving: An overview of charitable giving in India, Charities Aid Foundation (CAF), 2017: www.cafonline.org/docs/default-source/about-us-publications/caf-india-master-report.pdf

*Generation Share* demonstrates the power of Sharing. The change-makers show just what's possible – now it's your turn. What can you share? How can you make a difference?

This book has been made through love and sharing. Each copy purchased will feed and educate a girl at Aarti Naik's slum-based school in Mumbai and will plant a tree as part of the Eden Reforestation Project. *Generation Share* is made sustainably from waste materials and is compostable, so when you are done with it, please share, swap and recycle it, so that it too can be a ripple, inspire more positive change and help to unleash our unlimited Sharing potential, demonstrating further the power of Sharing to change the world.

Benita Matofska is an international public speaker, change-maker and world-leading expert on the Sharing Economy. An award-winning social entrepreneur, she created the charity The People Who Share and Global Sharing Week. Through social innovation, Benita helps organisations become change-makers and features regularly in the media worldwide.

**@benitamatofska**

Sophie Sheinwald is an award-winning visual storyteller who specialises in photography with purpose. Drawing on her background in fine arts, visual studies and community art, she combines her ability to connect with her passion to help people and businesses create meaningful, mission-driven brands.

**@sophie_snap**